My Mother, the Doctor

Joy Daniels Singer

MY MOTHER, THE DOCTOR

E. P. DUTTON & CO., INC. NEW YORK
1970

To Professor William M. Sale, Jr.
who taught me how to read a book,
and made it more likely I would write one.

And, of course, to Jack, who makes everything much
more likely.

Contents

8   *Contents*

My Mother, the Doctor

Apologia

MUCH OF THIS story came to me as folklore. It was told first by one person one time in one way, then by another in an entirely different way. It passed into my memory in bits and pieces that sorted out and arranged themselves. Also, much of it is childish memory. What Elka, my grandmother, told me I assimilated in pidgin Yiddish, since Elka died when I was nine, and would never speak English to me, though she understood it perfectly. [The reader will find a pidgin Yiddish glossary at the end of the book.]

As she scrubbed out an ear or washed a dirty foot, she would make up a rhyme about something that had happened years ago to her, or to my mother when she was still Hannahle. A nursery rhyme. And a nursery memory.

What my Aunt Mary told me comes from crowded rides back and forth in the car to Atlantic Beach, the only time Mary ever sat still long enough for reminiscence. So those tales came, garbled with admonitions to children to stop it, and frantic searches for a quarter for the Triborough Bridge.

And my mother's memories are marvelously elastic. They stretch to fit any number of circumstances, and sometimes the circumstances change so from one telling to another that I think I'm hearing an entirely new story.

So to those more expert than I in the facts of Borschevka and the *stetl* life, to those who know different stories or the same stories differently, and to those who object to the poetic license of memory, I can only say that this is only my truth, my Borschevka, my family, and my mother, the doctor.

Read it for what it is. It couldn't be anything else.

It Began in Borschevka

IT'S A TINY LITTLE TOWN, Borschevka, "the little hill of beets," in the Ukraine, near to Kiev, where my family history begins. And it's a pretty small family history, too. It only goes as far back as my grandparents, Elka Sirgutz, my grandmother, and "Reb Israel Ketointe" (Rabbi Israel, the small one), Israel Kleegman, my grandfather. At first, their union did not seem *beshert,* that wonderful Yiddish word that means fate and kismet and groovy, all at once. At first, indeed, it seemed fated only for disaster.

My Grandmother Elka was the village beauty, a tiny little girl with blue eyes and ringlets, whose gaiety and quick laughter were something of a *shunde,* a scandal in that community of so much sorrow and woe. From childhood she had eyes only for Chiam . . . a perfect match for her—tall, handsome, with grave brown eyes that seemed to foretell a future filled with purpose, and a destiny that would take them far away from starvation, pogroms, oppression, and sorrow. As children they talked of the new world . . . the world where gold lay in the streets, where anyone for free could go to school and learn anything, where only your imagination limited your horizons, where plain people from Borschevka, people they knew, went and earned eight dollars a week. It was true. It was no lie.

Didn't Elka's own best friend's sister, a girl too stupid and ugly to find a husband, go to Amerika and make eight dollars a week just sewing . . . and not even by hand, by machines!

Ah, yes. Chiam and Elka would marry, would go to Amerika, would work, and raise children who could all go to school and learn, and learn, and learn, *anything*. Professors they could be! Chiam and Elka would marry. No one ever thought any different. Who could?—looking at that golden couple, walking through the dimness of a Borschevka evening, and turning it alight with their love.

They only waited until Elka was fourteen to announce their engagement. Beautiful young Elka . . . strong, handsome Chiam would marry in a year, the year it took to prepare their home and to put into it the things that would last a marriage long . . . pots, homemade furniture, the cloths that Elka would sew on to make her family linens. Once they were married there would be no money for such frippery. Now was the time to be frivolous, to say, "This will stand here in the room, and that will go there."

But they forgot that if Elka was fifteen at her marriage, Chiam would be eighteen, and eighteen was the age when the Czar's army came to take you. Borschevka had been lucky. No recruiting squad from the Czar's army had come through recently. Perhaps it was so small as to be entirely forgotten.

Not so small, after all. The Czar's men came, they took, and one who was taken was Chiam. Well, so they wouldn't marry this year. It was a worrisome delay. After all, Elka at sixteen would be pretty old for a Borschevka bride. And the year of army service might change Chiam, might dim that golden youthfulness that made him so extraordinary, such a fine match for Elka. Only Elka never worried. She knew. She had been born for only one thing: to marry Chiam and raise children, beautiful children in a marvelous new world where everyone laughed and no one was ever poor. Chiam would come back, her Chiam, untouched and unchanged, ready to take up life again . . . their own wonderful life.

Chiam did come back, but only to die. The beautiful young man came home with a terrible cough, a cough so severe it won him his freedom from the Czar's army a full two months early. A cough so severe it was pneumonia, and took away with it the past and the future.

The whole town mourned. They were such a fine couple. But perhaps it wasn't ever wise for a Jew to be gay. To laugh the way Elka laughed. To see the future as a brilliant, glorious path to be run across . . . the way Elka and Chiam had run and danced.

The town poet made a song that the whole town sang. Like all Borschevka songs, it was a wailing melody, soft, minor, and mourning. The words were short, yet they told it all:

> *In the bride's home*
> *The wedding dress hangs,*
> *And not a movement, not a breath stirs it.*

> *On the grave of the groom*
> *The grasses grow tall.*
> *They are blowing in the strong autumn wind.*

But there was Elka with the rest of a life to live. And what could she do with it? No Chiam. No Amerika. No professor-children. Only Borschevka, Borschevka where life had no future, just an end.

Gone overnight was the gay young girl with ringlets. The ringlets fell out, and what grew back was hair shorter than the hair of the orthodox men of Borschevka. Gone were the blue eyes that tears washed out to a pale, red-rimmed gray. Gone were the purpose, the belief, the desire of Elka Sirgutz, village beauty no more, but just another one of the wailing women of Borschevka.

In despair her father and mother went to the village wise-men, the *rebs* of the *shul,* who spent all day studying Torah,

arguing Talmudic theory, and settling the problems of Borschevka as a sideline.

What could they do with Elka? She was sixteen; her life was
finished; she did nothing all day but weep. She, the singing
darling of their lives, never even spoke except to say *"Na, na"*
to everything they offered . . . trips, clothes, sweets, anything
their poor resources could bring forth.

The wise men counciled together. One did not have to be
gay in Borschevka. No one could force Elka to sing. A woman
of sixteen should have serious things to consider. Not a lost
love or a dead lover in a world where death was so ordinary.
She needed life and work and real trouble to take her mind off
her dreams. A husband, children, a home—those were the
answers, and it shouldn't take up the time of wise men for her
parents to see that. Find Elka a man, marry her off. Ah! But
here the wise men could help. There was no need for a matchmaker. The wise men of the *shul* themselves would make the
match. And what a match! What a smart man, a man with a
brain that could settle the knottiest problems . . . a man so
brilliant, so desirable that the *rebs* were bringing him all the
way from Austria, to be a personage in their *shul*. His name
was Israel Kleegman, and so good was God that Israel had actually asked them to find him a pious wife. There, what a
match! Made. Of course, Reb Israel was older; such a wise
head was not placed on young shoulders. But thirty-one was
not such an age; and, after all, Elka would need gentleness at
first, before she had children to love.

The wise men turned back to the Talmud, wishing the
problems of words were as easy to solve as the problems of people. People—you could tell them what to do, and they
obeyed. Words just stayed there on the page, refusing to
change their meaning or even to clarify it, no matter what the
needs of the interpreters.

Elka's parents went home. Maybe it wasn't perfect, but at
least they would have grandchildren. And Elka couldn't stay

like this, the way they found her, the household left to itself, nothing cooked, nothing washed or clean, and Elka lying, lying staring face up without even seeing the ceiling. It was done. It was a match. But who would tell her?

Yet there was a surprise in store for her desperate parents. When her father told her roughly to get up and stop thinking of Chiam because she would soon have another man to think about, she did not weep or wail. Her eyes, it is true, stayed fixed to the ceiling, but she did not complain, not even with the *"Na, na"* they were accustomed to.

She looked at the ceiling, and none know what she saw—certainly not her mother or father. But she accepted her fate with one word and no more. *"Schon."* Okay. For Elka, now, one life was as good as another, or maybe as bad. Without Chiam she had no dreams. But her dreams had been real to her, as this life would never be. Best get it lived, best get on with it.

She rose from her bed to assume a woman's burden. She asked no questions about Israel Kleegman. Who could he be in her life? A stranger who had never shared a hope with her. Nor linked fingers racing down a hill. She would live her life by herself, no matter who was alongside. He couldn't be Chiam. He could only be nothing.

The wedding preparations went along. All the beautiful linens and sturdy chairs were placed, not by lovers who had walked over every piece of floor and paced out every wall, but by villagers who put down and ran out. Elka had her short curls shaven to put on the *shaittel,* the wig of the married Jewish woman. She went to the ritual bath, the *mikveh,* and was cleansed for her husband.

It was her wedding day. With that same steady stare, she walked through the village streets, on the arm of her father, to meet her husband, a man who arrived just that day. Even her father had only seen him once, at the signing of the marriage agreement. And what can a man say of another to a young girl?

"He's a good man. A fine brain, he has. God grant he will be kind to you." But what had God granted her so far? She stared ahead, and wouldn't think of anything but one foot and then another, moving them, moving them to the *shul.*

At the *shul* she walked to the *hoopah,* the canopy under which she stood with the rabbi, her parents, and someone else, someone she never raised her eyes to see. She heard the prayers, heard the cries of *Mazeltov* as the glass was broken under someone's foot, and then walked away, grabbing again for her father's arm to hold her up.

In the room where the wedding feast was laid, she sat watching the dancers, listening to the toasts given for health and happiness and long, long life to the blessed couple. She played perfectly the part of the bride. She was silent and well behaved. Her eyes stayed cast down. Her feet never moved to the temptation of the music. At last the guests began to leave. The people of the village, the strangers who had come from far away to celebrate the marriage of the bridegroom. One by one they left, striding feet, shuffling feet, young feet, old feet.

At last there was a quick kiss on the cheek, and her mother's voice whispering a soft encouragement, her father's deep tones uttering a benediction . . . and then there was only one pair of feet, in black shoes, far away across the room.

She raised her eyes. There he was. It must be he; there was no one else left. But *Oi Guttenu,* O dear God, was this what she got instead of Chiam? This tiny little man scarcely bigger than she was, with his little monkey face and his slanted eyes that made him look as though he were squinting at the light, even in the dim candles of the room. This man with his big beard and little shoulders, who was smiling pleasantly at her and who said, "Elka?"

As he rose from his seat to walk toward her, she tried, she really tried. But it was, O dear God, too much. She fainted dead away.

So much the family history tells about Elka and Israel and

their first meeting. So much my grandmother Elka told. But what was never told is what happened after the faint, and how—in the few short weeks after their marriage—Israel comforted her and cozened her and coaxed her to become gay again, and to think about the real life she would lead with him. Certainly it is part of family legend that she was so besotted with him in the early years that the whole town chastised her for worrying so much about her husband and so little about her children . . . and when Israel was an old man he undertook a trip by train and bus into *goy* country (the deepest South) because, he said, he had been too long away from Elka —who was visiting Hannahle, my mother—and he wanted her in bed! He blamed it on a stricture of the Talmud, but he said it with the gleam of a lover in his eyes.

Enter Hannable

OF COURSE this was a pre-Revolutionary Russia, a country that denied even the Industrial Revolution and brought into the twentieth century a serfdom other countries had outgrown in the eighteenth. The Russian peasant was, though freed by statute, still a slave—to the Czar, to the nobility, to the land, and to the natural and unnatural catastrophes that beset him —hourly, daily, yearly. His farming methods were the methods of Cain and Abel . . . and his brotherly love was arrested at about the same level. It was not so much a hand-to-mouth existence as a tooth-to-tooth existence. Where the land could not provide for the people, each had to wrest what he could from his fellowman. Everyone was poor in Borschevka. But the Jews were poorer than anybody. What they had was fair game for everyone. The Czar might decide to seize property from the Jews. The district might decide to seize from the Jews, the mayor might decide to seize from the Jews, and the peasants might decide to seize from the Jews. This was in normal or "good times." In bad times an official pogrom was proclaimed, and it was everyone's *duty* to seize from the Jews.

And, since they lived in Borschevka and in a ghetto, Elka and Israel's life was far from ideal. The ghetto was not walled

in by bricks, but only by an instinct for survival. It was a large
group of small buildings huddled together, about two miles
away from the "town" of Borschevka. The "town" consisted of
five or six buildings that housed all the officialdom of the
village—town hall, church, shops, school. The peasants of
Borschevka were farmers. Their homes were spread out over a
ten- or twelve-mile area. On shopping days, on feast days, and
on rare Sundays they came into town. Officials had twenty or
thirty towns like Borschevka to visit, and made those visits
once a month, or once every two months, to keep the townspeople in touch with their responsibilites to the Czar.

So Elka and Israel lived in the ghetto, a huddle of buildings
in the realm of the Angel of Death. And death was familiar to
all the Jews of Borschevka. Elka's eleven children showed little of her own gift for survival against cruel fate. Six boys died,
one after the other, of no food, no medicine, and no *koyech,*
the uniquely Jewish stamina that enabled any of the Jews to
live. Four of the five girls survived, but what were girls in a
Jewish family?

Still, Elka never abandoned her dreams. There was another
world, another way to live. If now they were wiser, and knew
that gold didn't really lie loose in the streets, still even girls
could become professors, in Amerika, to teach the children of
everybody, Jew and Gentile alike. And if you had only girls,
shouldn't you go where they can learn like men? Especially
such marvelous girls as hers . . . Meriam, Rachel, Hannahle
. . . Ah, Hannahle, what a treasure! And Hannahle, of course,
became my mother. Not the oldest, not the last, but the one
who had Elka's gaiety and Israel's wisdom . . . and an inborn
knowledge of the world possessed by neither parent, but her
own gift from the gods.

Poor Hannahle was a twin . . . a three-pound miracle of
koyech. But when she was born, no one mentioned her. They
never said there were twins. Or that a girl was born. There
were only great celebration and rejoicing over her twin

brother . . . a boy, a boy who weighed very little, but who counted for so much. What a beauty! See. His mother's eyes and a head of hair! What preparations there were for the *briss,* the ritual circumcision of a Jewish boy! But when the guests came, there was no *briss.* So quickly, the boy was dead. All that was left was this shriveled little girl. "No bigger than a tablespoon," marveled the women. "Well, the next meeting should be for a happier occasion," said the men. That was the last time the family ever mourned that they had been left with Hannahle . . . her father's treasure, her mother's golden hands.

Even girls had to eat. Israel was the village wise man; everyone loved and respected Reb Israel Ketointe, the little man with the enormous understanding. But being wise paid off only in respect, not food. After Reb Israel would run throughout the village to the baker, the butcher, the chicken farmer to beg food and money, he would come home triumphant to Elka.

"Look, Elka, look. I have six kopeks, two loaves, and twenty chicken feet for the starving children, the poor children of Borschevka. I must go, I must give it out at the *shul.*"

Elka would say in despair, "But, Israel, we have nothing to eat right here. Give me something for our children."

"Our children, Elka, our children don't starve. The Lord provides for them."

And he would come home happily to his dinner of potatoes and pickled cucumbers, the best Elka could spread in her home. It was true, none of the children actually starved, but Elka got tired of waiting for the Lord to provide. Though the Lord might love those who helped others, she wanted to help herself.

One skill she had she was already using among her neighbors and friends. She was an expert herbalist, and knew the properties of the local plants, those that cured and those that strengthened and those that could make a potato and onion stew taste like food for a feast.

She decided to set up a little store. There was a room in her mother's house she could use, a back room that had its own door. She started with herbs that she went far into the fields to find. Among the local Russian peasants, the *goyim,* there was always great demand for love potions and aphrodisiacs. She also put in a supply of tobacco, and finally she found that she could make money from the skill of her hands, so she treated simple ailments as well. It was the closest thing Borschevka had to a real shop. For what could they buy with no money? But in the wintertime there was a fire going in the store, even if there wasn't one at home. The peasant men took it as a place to come to after a day's work. They would sit around a table in the middle of the tiny room and play cards and drink liquor they had brought themselves, and pay my grandmother for the privilege of sitting there.

Round the table would go the bottle; round the table the cards were dealt. The men brought with them what little money they made at work. They sat inside as warm and comradely as only a Russian peasant can be. And inside sat my grandmother, Elka, looking out the door to the winter outside. There would appear one face and then another at the door. The faces of the wives outside. "Please give me money before you gamble. Just enough for food, only enough to eat." The cries were always the same, and always drowned by the laughter of the men.

While Elka lived, never, no, never, could we sit around the table and play cards, even in the warmth of a summer day. Even in golden Amerika.

Saccbareen

WHILE ELKA kept the shop, Israel had one great commercial triumph each year. The year Hannah was five she was to share it with him. What a sign of favor! This was the year Hannah would go with her father to market to sell the *kvass*. *Kvass* was the local soft drink. It was made from fruit—berries, pears, apples—and was sold at the country fair. But since it was a drink for women and children, and did not offer escape or even stimulation, it was a rare treat. The men were allowed their Saturday-night drunk; *kvass* was only for very special occasions.

It was a very small hut that the family called home. One of the beds was just a shelf over the stove. That was the best bed, because it was so narrow only one person (even if it was a very small person) could sleep in it. And it was always a little warmer than the rest of the house, for the stone mantel, which was—after all—the bedstead, retained heat.

It was an even smaller hut during the months before market. Then it was hung with drying apples. Apple strings swung from the low ceiling. Hannah, who was so tiny, could still run through the rooms. But anyone over three feet tall stooped under the drying apples, moving carefully from string to string so as not to bring down the whole Kleegman economy on their heads.

The apples had to dry out very slowly. The heat in the house had to be kept constant. And when the whole family went out on a search for wood to burn in the fireplace, they were braving the Ukrainian snows and winds, not for themselves, but to keep the apples drying, to make Reb Israel's *kvass* have the true taste.

As pious a man as Reb Israel created his *kvass* as a work of the Lord, a celebration of the goodness of the earth and its yield. Again and again he would tell Hannah how only the purest of nature's harvests were good enough. His apples were the finest apples, sorted over and over. Indeed, Hannah was to go to market with him because it was she who had the keenest eye for a wormhole or a blemish when the apples were chosen. No matter how much Elka would mutter or exclaim that this apple was good enough, Reb Israel and Hannah would look again and shake their heads together. For Reb Israel's *kvass,* only the perfect could be chosen.

Elka would go and gather special herbs, the subtle flavorings that only she could find. Weeks ahead of time she brought them home so they could dry, too, and be ready when the apples were. Then the huge caldrons were scrubbed and scoured, buried half in the earth to make sure that no matter how hard the children stirred they could not tip over the *kvass* and let it spill to the ground.

The apples were pressed through a giant sieve that took three people to turn it. Most important of all, the good sugar was pounded from lumps into grains and then poured in by Reb Israel's unstinting hand. Sugar in Borschevka . . . ah, that was a luxury. What munificence to actually pour it out in a steady stream! For sugar was meted out, a tiny, tiny bit at a time by Elka. No one poured sugar into the tea to sweeten it. You held a precious lump between your teeth, trying desperately to keep it from melting too fast. You drank the tea around the lump, savoring each second of sweetness . . . and then you only remembered the taste; the sugar was all gone.

But Reb Israel was a true profligate with his *kvass*. He poured in the sugar. He poured in more. He tasted. Yes, still more. And his *kvass* was the best anywhere around Borschevka. When children begged for a treat at the fair, it was never just any treat; it was a glass of Reb Israel's *kvass*.

The *kvass* was made. Now it went into the ground to "grow" before time for market, keeping cool in the mild Ukrainian spring. Something Elka put in it kept it from fermenting, and something about the maturing process gave it a glow that makes every Ukrainian talk about *kvass* with the sadness of one remembering a vintage long gone, never again to be savored in this life.

Hannah had waited and waited. As the strings of apples dried, it was forever in her five-year-old world. As the apples were sieved and the sugar poured in, she couldn't understand the terrible patience of her mother and father. But it was time, oh, now it was really time. The day of the fair was come. Only today was the *kvass* siphoned into the barrels, kept all year only to hold *kvass*. Five beautiful barrels filled with *kvass* to go to the fair. The barrels were loaded onto a wagon. A neighbor's mule, bespoken months before, was hitched to it.

But the beast, accustomed as he was to overloading, could barely pull that full, full wagon through the ruts of the road. The terrible cold had left. Now there was only the terrible mud. Hannahle followed Reb Israel into the damp chill of two o'clock in the morning. There was a six-hour walk to the marketplace where the spring fair would be held. The rest of the family could wait and come later, in a wagon drawn by two horses—loaned by a rich uncle once a year for the fair. But valuable horses could not be risked hauling *kvass,* so Hannahle and Reb Israel made their long, necessary head start.

How long, O Lord, was that walk as Reb Israel stopped to say his ceremonial prayers, as he added one or two out of his private joy at taking the fruits of his labors to market. This was a great occasion for him. A man who had only the mechanism of his mind to offer the Lord, the questionings and involutions of a blind believer, was able at last to offer up something that could be touched and tasted. Hannah walked beside him, not noticing the miles or the cold. His pure joy transfigured them both. Hand in hand, often outpacing the poor mule that Reb Israel led, they brought God's goodness to market.

And in the market Reb Israel led with a sure hand. His place was hallowed to him. No one else would dare to trespass on it. For once he was made way for not only as a wise man and one they could look up to. Reb Israel was good business. A place next to him was worth money. For everyone who came to the fair made their way to Reb Israel's little stall. It was not only the *kvass*, although that was surely the best to be found in all of Borschevka, in all the Ukraine, and, those who had been to Moscow said, in all the world . . . but Reb Israel had a word here, an answer there. You would just pass the time of day with him, answer his polite questions about yourself and your family, and suddenly find that you had solved your problem, the weight of it seemed to have dropped from your shoulders.

How did he do it? A gentle remark, so quiet it hardly seemed like a suggestion, a quote from the Talmud. It was not as if he told you what to do; after all, you hadn't even asked him. It was just that everything seemed to flow more smoothly when you talked to Reb Israel.

This first visit Hannah made, in her own fifth year, was a year that was never forgotten. It was the year of the new inspector. Hannahle watched, fascinated, as Reb Israel went to his usual place and began to set things up for a busy day. Hannahle had never seen more than the few people of her village gathered together in one place. She was thrilled with the hubbub of the marketplace. The yells, the greetings, the loud complaints, the protests of the wagon wheels unused to long journeys, all sounded in her ears as a familiar hum, magnified by some majestic force to a thousand times its usual volume. Gradually the loud noise worked itself into a pattern. The greetings were over and it was time to talk. Who better to come to in fear and worry than Reb Israel?

First this one, then another came up to them.

"A new Inspector this year."

"Oi, bist ir a gonif!"

"Inspector Borlovsky is gone. Never did I think to miss him."

"Inspectors, inspectors. In the earth should they all be buried!"

The swell of complaint was high. The usual tragedies of undutiful wives, ungrateful children, and unfruitful labors were all drowned in this new threat to their existence.

For the Inspector was a personage. He had the power—absolute and without recourse—to destroy an entire year's efforts. His authority was without limit. What Jew could complain about him? Who would even hear such a complaint? On the Inspector, benevolent or despotic, they all depended. Inspector Borlovsky was a devil they knew. What about the new inspector?

His ostensible reason for existence was to protect the health of the community, and his title was Health Inspector. In an area where a whole family's work was brought to one fair a year to be sold, the Health Inspector of that fair had powers of life and death. A bad year at the fair meant no money for food for the winter. No sales meant that children would die of hunger. And the Health Inspector could declare your goods a health hazard. That was all. Foodstuffs that seemed not quite fresh were a health hazard. By some strange stretch of the laws of the Czar, even badly sewn clothes were a health hazard. The Health Inspector passed on all. And all needed the blessing of his nod.

And the Health Inspector kept a very special watch for the

greatest hazard of all—the terrible act of poisoning food with saccharin. It was well known at that time in Russia that saccharin was as deadly as arsenic. It led to wasting diseases, made your hair and teeth fall out, caused goiter, cancer, and less mentionable ailments. But it sweetened the food cheaply, unlike expensive sugar, so that unscrupulous merchants who didn't mind poisoning their customers were likely to slip it into desserts, candy, and drink. The Health Inspector's cry of "Sacchareen" was his most absolute decree. He needed a very sensitive palate so that he could detect at a taste the degree and quality of sweetness.

And on the Inspector's delicate palate depended the Kleegman family's well-being. With Inspector Borlovsky, Reb Israel had had a relationship of respect tempered on each side by condescension. Each was a big man to the community. Each wielded great power, power that was absolute. That Reb Israel's power was not accompanied by the power of the Czar didn't matter. His word was law amongst the *rebs* of the *shul*. And their word was the last word in the Borschevka ghetto.

Inspector Borlovsky might have the power of the Czar behind him. Reb Israel could summon up the Talmud and all the ecclesiastical arguments.

But now Inspector Borlovsky was no more. There was a new Inspector.

Like any unknown quantity within that tightly defended community, the new Inspector was a threat. In Borschevka xenophobia was not an aberration; it was a necessary defense.

"Don't worry," said Reb Israel, a man who knew the responsibilities of power, "an Inspector is an important man. He'll do us no harm. We aren't important enough to trouble him. After all, no matter what, Inspector Borlovsky would always listen to reason. A little talk, a little joke, a little taste. You'll see. A big man from the Czar won't bother to upset our little fair."

But the big man from the Czar had his own ideas. This job

was his as a sinecure. He expected each little Borschevkan (after all, it is only Borschevka that concerns us, but the fair contained perhaps the people of fifty Borschevkas, a regular world's fair) and each little townsman to contribute to his personal well-being. A kopek here, a kopek there. It was all money in the pocket. And, as luck would have it, he came to Reb Israel's stand the first one.

"Come in, come in, Inspector," said Reb Israel. "Please, come in, taste, taste. Try the *kvass*. It is the purest drink of God's goodness. Please, taste, enjoy." Reb Israel was not immodest. He was pleased that God had given him something good to create. Even Hannahle was pleased. Her father was a great man, able to offer refreshment fit for a representative of the Czar. She was more pleased when her father poured for the Inspector, and a tiny glass for her.

They all drank. Reb Israel savored his work, and it was good. Hannahle drank her drink, and it was nectar, the food of all gods. But the big man from the Czar had his own ideas. He didn't taste so quickly. Reb Israel took away the glass. In some way he had offended the new Inspector.

With great ceremony he wiped off another glass. He smiled confidently, deprecatingly at the new Inspector. He turned the spigot again, and the golden *kvass* poured out of the barrel. With great dignity Reb Israel offered a fresh glass to the new inspector.

"Drink," said Reb Israel "drink in health and happiness."

The new Inspector raised the glass to his lips. Reb Israel waited for the praise he knew would be forthcoming. Inspector Borlovsky had always closed his eyes, savored that first sip on his tongue, and then uttered his final accolade: "Yes, ye-e-e-es."

The new Inspector tasted. He rolled the *kvass* around in his mouth. Suddenly he spat it out on the ground. What kind of tasting was this? What way to treat Reb Israel's *kvass*? Oh, there, he took another mouthful. Four eyes watched anxiously. Why did the Inspector's face stay twisted in a look of disdain? Why had it not relaxed into enjoyment?

"M-m-m-m-m-m," said the new Inspector, "to me it tastes, perhaps, now just perhaps, of saccharin." He waited. He had played the first part of the game. It was Reb Israel's turn to play the next . . . the game of maybe, oh-no, my kopeks say no, played by the petty officialdom of the Czar.

Reb Israel was a wise man and a good man . . . about the troubles of his people he knew everything . . . about the poverty of a little village-fair Inspector, nothing . . . and about the corruption of the world—even less. To him the Inspector was a big man, a man making a judgment. And who was being judged? Not only Reb Israel, but the good Lord himself, the good Lord who had helped Reb Israel pick the apples, who had blessed the *kvass*. That his *kvass*, that great collaboration between Israel and the Lord, should be questioned! Would Israel poison his people, people who trusted him, with *saccharin?* Reb Israel was overtaken by the terribleness of the accusation. Tears fell from his eyes and protests from his lips. Out came the words . . . word after word in more and more learned Hebrew phrases, all completely incomprehensible to the new Inspector . . . proof after proof from the Talmud, beautifully constructed and intoned. Even in Reb Israel's anguish he could not abandon the elegance of argument.

Hannah listened. She understood the Inspector. After all, Reb Israel knew the law of the Torah, but Hannah made change in the store. She knew the Russians very well. Didn't they try hard to cheat her when they laughed and watched the baby make change? "Father," said Hannahle, *"sha, sha."* She couldn't reach much further than his coat skirt, but she pulled as hard as she could on that. "Father, he wants money. Give him some money." When Hannahle saw he would not listen, she tried again. "Father, for money he will like the *kvass.*"

"What do you know, Hannah? Go away. *Gay avec,* this is a

matter for men. Money! He says I'm a poisoner . . . that my
kvass, my beautiful *kvass* is poison. Go away. Go away. Money.
You shame your father."

The new Inspector watched and listened. The girl and her
father were talking about *gelt. Gelt* he understood; that meant
money. But things were not going right, and he could not
allow this to happen. His power was all-powerful, and he must
prove it once and for all. This was the first time; it had to be
the last time there would be any questioning of his authority.
Once more he took the taste of *kvass* in his mouth. This time
he barely allowed it to touch his lips before he spat it out like
venom, far away.

His voice rose. It lost its confidential tones. No longer was
he going to make it easy for the *reb,* a transaction between gentlemen of a confidential nature. The Inspector wanted everyone to see. Everyone must hear. "I am sure now. My tongue is
never wrong." His voice rose to a mighty shout. Thus might
doomsday smite the ears of the doomed:

"SACCHA-*REEN*."

And with that roar he strode over to the cart, to the six barrels, gaily decorated. He pulled hard. Out came the first bung
. . . then the next, then the next. At last all six barrels bled
onto the muddy road.

The people watched. They turned from the shame of the
reb. Politeness took them away, as well as discretion. And into
each hand crept a tribute for the new Inspector. Well enough,
they had learned that lesson.

Reb Israel watched until the last drop of *kvass* had sunk
into the ground. He held Hannahle's hand. But no word did
he say. Even after the donkey was hitched again to the cart and
the journey back was begun, he said nothing. Hannah tried
again. She thought it might be comfort, and she knew it was
truth. "Father, he only wanted money." But Reb Israel said
nothing. Not even *"Sha."* Only once did words pass his lips

that whole trip back. And then it was only two words. What terrible words. "A poisoner."

The next year Elka pulled Hannahle aside. Women knew why the world went on instead of stopping in its tracks. Elka put ten kopeks in Hannahle's hand. No instructions were given. Hannahle didn't need them. When the new Inspector came again to Reb Israel's stall, again this year the first thing, Hannahle ran out to meet him. "Good day, Inspector"; she said it in Russian, and curtsied. As she dropped that curtsy, she managed also to drop the kopeks in his hand. That year the new Inspector drained the first glass of *kvass* at a gulp, and asked for a second glass, which he savored. His humor was good. His attitude toward the *reb* even jolly. The one black sheep returned to the fold makes you ever more grateful. And this year Reb Israel had made no fuss about the bribe; indeed, it had been given gracefully, by a little charmer who spoke Russian.

But for Reb Israel, something of the goodness of God had deserted his *kvass*.

That year when Hannahle was five was altogether a terrible year for the Kleegmans, and for all the Borschevka ghetto. Borschevka seemed to have called down on itself the notice of officialdom. First, the new Inspector . . . then, what they all dreaded, the pogrom. So insignificant was Borschevka that—as they had once before thought they would be overlooked when the Czar's men came looking for soldiers—now they thought: we're not important enough to persecute . . . we're only Borschevka.

But it was trouble enough to be only Borschevka. That dreadful year. It was an awful winter. Cold, they didn't remember such a cold. And then to the Kleegmans came the measles. Hannahle had it, a light case, but enough to give it to Rachel. And poor Rachel, Elka said she didn't *have* the measles; she *was* a measle. Then, as Rachel slept in the choice bed, the stone mantel over the fireplace, turning in the bitter cold, hot with a raging fever, there was a tap at the door, a very gentle tap. Only Elka heard it. It was the middle of the night; it couldn't be a customer for the store, but she ran quickly to open up before Rachel was wakened. There was a customer, an old peasant whose wife she had saved during another winter and a different epidemic. "Come out of the cold. Come, come in," said Elka.

"No, no" said the old man, "you must come out, and quickly. The soldiers are in the Russian town; there will be a pogrom. There is no time to argue, and no time to stay. Run out, now, before they get here."

"But Rachel is burning up with fever. How can she go out, how can any of us go out in this cold?"

"Rachel is twelve, almost thirteen. You want to keep her here for a pogrom? There is no time. Come, come now, come out and hide in the woods until they go. I can help you no more. I, too, must run. If they find me with you, it will be no better for me."

So Elka woke Israel and the girls. They took everything they could find to wrap around Rachel, whose fever was so high she was barely conscious, and they carried her out. Run, run they did—feet bare, for who had time to wrap the rags around that served as shoes? Out into the woods with burning Rachel. And there they stayed the whole night, as the soldiers stormed from one house to another, breaking everything . . . throwing everyone out into the cold, in a mass roundup of Borschevkans, everyone but a girl here and another there whom they kept warm inside the house.

In the morning Borschevka, the ghetto, had been turned inside out. Every possession thrown into the snow. Houses took too long to knock down, but windows were all gone, doors torn away and burned. And people had disappeared, too. One family lost a daughter, another a husband. No one knew exactly why they took Jews away in a pogrom. And no one knew what happened to the ones that disappeared.

Hannahle remembered only how she and Rachel huddled together in Israel's arms, and how Rachel's body was so hot, Hannahle expected to have scars from the burns. Rachel survived her measles and her night. But for two years she could not talk above a whisper, and for all her life she was deaf. Very deaf at first. Then not so deaf. Then very deaf again.

Hannah—Der Kleine Wunder

HANNAH BEGAN STOREKEEPING at three. The value of a kopek was impressed on her at a very early age, and her ability to give change with lightning-like speed delighted the whole town. They would come in and buy some small item with a big coin just for the pleasure of seeing the tiny cashier place it carefully in the cashbox, poke around quickly with a grubby forefinger, and give back the right amount without ever making a mistake. *"A kleine wunder,"* the ghetto people said admiringly— and a little wonder she was indeed.

Hannah was never frightened by the rough voices of the peasants or their rather heavy-handed jokes. If a peasant man said to her, "Little one, don't you want to sit in my pocket? I'll take you for a nice long ride." Her answer was likely to be, "No, sir, and you'd like it better if you took this nice package of tobacco. It's fine tobacco . . . and it will fit better there than I would." More often than not, she would make an extra sale. Few people could resist Hannah's ready sales pitch.

Among the patrons of the store were the peasant children, who came in to find their fathers and beg a few pennies for sweets. Hannah looked with envy at their books. Real books in Russian, some even with pictures. These were not like the prayer books from which she read so painfully. These taught you things about the world. She was already learning to speak Russian with her customers, although Russian was a language frowned on in the ghetto. But she couldn't read or write it, and Borschevka was not likely to give her the chance to come across a Russian grammar.

The peasant children went to the Russian school. The Jewish children studied in the ghetto. If they were man-children they studied long and hard, learning the intricacies of Torah and Talmud. But what they studied kept them firmly within the ghetto; it didn't open up the outside world, the world that, even at three or four, was the world Hannah knew waited for her.

Diligently she learned everything she could from the store. One kopek and one kopek made two kopeks, that she could see for herself. And a tobacco package that cost ten kopeks plus a bag of sweets for one kopek meant eleven kopeks in the strongbox. Two packages of tobacco were twenty kopeks, and so it went. Arithmetic had to be her strongest subject at the store-school.

Elka had started early with each of the girls to talk about the marvels of that new world of her dreams. She said again and again: "In Amerika you could learn anything . . . even girls. I'm telling you. Girls go to school there forever, just like the men here. And it's free. You don't pay. You just work hard and learn what you like."

Elka was content just to think about a faraway future in the new world, content to build the idea in the minds of her daughters. But not Hannah. Hannah listened. Hannah understood that none of them could be sure of getting an education unless they moved to the new world. And Reb Israel would listen to Elka's talk about "When we go to Amerika . . . in Amerika . . . when we can get to Amerika," but as far as Hannah could see—and she understood her father very well—he showed no intention of ever going there. He was content to let Elka have her dream. It wasn't his dream, too.

No, she would have to get her education here and now. She did not want a religious education. She wanted a Russian education. The abstruse passages of Talmudic instruction did not interest her. Leave that to the boys who were made so welcome in the *shul*. She had to go to Russian school. But how?

The Russian school did not take the Jewish children even if their parents wanted them to come. It was very difficult for a Jew to get in, and required all kinds of official permissions. And no Jewish girls went to the school. The peasant boys were quite grown up, the peasant girls very willing, and the pious elders of the synagogue were under no illusions about what went on under the trees during recess. It was no place for a nice Jewish girl. Besides, no child from the Borschevka ghetto, boy or girl, had ever been permitted to go to the Russian school. The ghetto took care of its own, but it kept them its own.

Hannah thought and thought. She was already five, and if she was to start at the proper age, at six, she had to begin. First, she had to convince Elka that she could be educated right here, right in Borschevka. Next, she had to be smart enough to get into the school.

She began with Elka.

"Mother, I want to go to school. Not to *shul* but to real school."

"Yes, yes, Hannahle, all my girls will go to real school. When we go to Amerika, you will become professors and learn and learn and teach and teach."

"No, Mother, not in Amerika. Here. Next year."

"But, Hannahle, what school can you go to? In the Russian school there are no Jews, and where else is there?"

"Yes, Mother. In the Russian school there can be Jews. Doesn't my cousin Ytsek go to a fine Russian gymnasium?"

"But, Hannah, that's in Moscow. And do you know what

they pay for him to go to that school? I can't send you to Moscow; I can't pay a kopek. Wait till we get to Amerika."

"In Amerika I'll be too far behind, Mother. I have to start right here, right now. Otherwise I'll never learn enough to become a professor. I'll just sew on shirts on a machine."

Elka looked at her baby girl. Suddenly she hugged her. "*Schon.*" Okay. Elka was convinced. And what Elka and Hannahle wanted, it took a great deal to keep them from getting.

Elka spoke to one of the old peasant men, one of her favorites among the customers. "Could you talk a little more with Hannahle? You know, tell her those fables you are always telling, the stories of Krilov. She wants to be able to speak Russian to the customers. Teach her what you can." The old Russian was a famous storyteller. He loved the stories of Krilov, the Russian Aesop; he loved children, and above all he loved Hannahle. Over and over he told her his favorites, the stories that the children had to learn in school. Soon she could tell them as well as he did, with even more energy and dramatic oratory.

Especially they loved the tale of the wolf and the crane and the bone that was stuck in the wolf's throat.

"Be off with you!" Hannahle would yell in her deepest, most wolflike tones, and in the heavily accented Russian of the local peasantry. "Be off with you, and be sure you never cross my path again!" Soon people were urging her to recite for them; and, never one to disappoint her audience, she would perch up on the table beside the cashbox, reciting one history or another, and solemnly pointing the moral with an outstretched fingertip.

But her purpose was much more serious than dramatic recitation. Her Russian was becoming more fluent, but time was passing, her sixth birthday approaching, and she still hadn't gotten any closer to the Russian school.

Elka said: "Patience, patience." But Hannahle's observation of life had not taught her that patience was any virtue.

"Mother, I'm going to talk to Father," she said determinedly.

"Go ahead; it won't help, but it won't hurt," said Elka.

So Hannahle began talking the next time she went along with her father to walk him to *shul*.

"Father," she said, "do I do the keeping of the store well?"

"Wonderfully well, *tauchterle*," he said.

"Father," she said, "I want to go to school."

"Well," he said musingly, "it's unusual, but I'll tell you Hannahle, I'll talk to the *rebs*. Such a smart girl as you, maybe they would let you study specially in the *shul*."

"No, Father, *not* in the *shul;* I want to go to the Russian school."

"Hannahle, never talk to me about this again."

"Yes, Father," said Hannah.

But not for nothing was Hannah Elka's daughter. One of the things Hannah had learned at her mother's elbow was if you want something you have to keep after it. What you can't get from people by kindness you can sometimes get by exasperating them. And what you can't get by exasperating them you can simply make a fact of life.

"Father," she said for the fiftieth time, "I want to go to Russian school."

"There's no question of your going, Hannahle," he stated firmly and finally. "Look at all the reasons you can't go. First, they don't take Jews in our Russian school. Second, if they did take Jews, you would have to pay to go and we don't have a kopek to pay for it. Third, if they did take Jews and we could pay for it, a gentle Jewish girl like you could not mix with the *huzzadiche* peasants. Fourth, if they did take Jews and we could pay for it, and you could keep yourself away from those rude peasant boys, the *rebs* would never allow anyone from our ghetto to go there. And, fifth, I told you never to talk to me about this again."

Hannah began to feel hopeful. For the first time, Reb Israel was giving her concrete objections, so he must have been considering the whole proposition.

"Besides," he said, "you would have to go to classes on Saturday. That is required at the Russian school. And that's the most serious problem of all. What can you do about the days of the week? Go to the Russians and get them to change the classes on *Shabbus,* and then, maybe, we can talk about it some more. Until then, I forbid you to mention this subject to me again."

Not for nothing had Reb Israel lived so many years with Elka. Let Hannah nag someone else for a change.

Hannah was beginning to worry. Her birthday was approaching; the problem of the *Shabbus* was the first that seemed to her insurmountable; and, persistent as she could be, what her father said was true: she couldn't change the days of the week.

School started without Hannah. Her birthday came and went. Well, she thought, I have a whole year to plan. I can work very hard next year and perhaps catch up on some of the lost time. It was her first academic defeat. It would prove to be the last.

As she worried over the problem of the *Shabbus,* the solution came to her. She would take her lessons home with her and work on them on Sunday when there was no school for Christians. She would be such a good student that her teachers wouldn't mind excusing her from the Saturday classes. All it meant was hard work, and for Hannah, hard work was easy.

She went back to her father.

"Father, I've worked it out. I make you a solemn promise. I won't go to school on the *Shabbus.*"

"And you won't write on the *Shabbus?* Remember, it is a sin to write on the day the Lord gave us to rest."

"No, Father, I promise now that I will never write on the *Shabbus,* if only you will let me go to Russian school."

(So solemn did she consider that promise, that even in later

years, when she was a full-fledged physician, as long as her
father lived she never wrote on a Saturday except to save a
life.)

"But, Hannah," said Reb Israel, realizing that he was beginning to weaken, and somewhat stunned by the enormity of
the step his baby daughter was taking, "what about all the rest?
Can you get into the Russian school? I don't think so. Can you
get them to take you without money? I don't think so. Can you
keep yourself away from the peasant boys, and stay a good and
pious Jewess? I don't think so. . . ."

"Father," she said, "all that I can do. I promise you, you will
have nothing but pride if you send me to the Russian school. I
will be the one to show them all what we can do in our little
ghetto in Borschevka. You'll see, I'll work well. I'll get good
marks. I'll bring home the honor certificate. But, Father, can
you make the *rebs* let me go to the Russian school?"

"Ah, this, I think so!"

Still, it proved to be a big task for Reb Israel. The *rebs* of
the *shul* listened to him in shocked disapproval. That Reb Israel should suggest sending his own daughter away from the
protection of the community into the stronghold of the
goyim! God alone knew what she might learn there, but it
wouldn't be anything helpful to a good Jewish *maidele*. Already she could do sums that would bewilder many an older
and wiser head. Already she amazed strangers with her learning, a little girl of only six. What more did she need? They put
their heads together, with much argument and then vigorous
nodding. Smilingly they came to the *reb*. They were prepared
to do much. Since he had no boy to carry on his tradition of
great learning, they would be willing to stretch tradition to its
utmost. Reb Israel could send Hannahle to the *shul* school.

"No. No. I thank you for your kindness, but it will not do. I
don't want my Hannahle to be always ashamed that she isn't a
boy. Such a wonderful child should not have to apologize for

anything. She is right and we are wrong. She must learn to live in more of a world than Borschevka."

Just then a much more serious problem took over the minds of the Borschevka elders. Anti-Semitism, which always had been prevalent in their Russia, now became more menacing. Planned pogroms erupted all over the Ukraine. The Ukraine was filled with the contagion of "Kill the Jews . . . death to the Jews." For six months it was a plague, and then it seemed to die down a little.

The elders came together. They decided to send a petition to the Czar—a long list of the persecutions they were faced with. For months, they argued over it word by word and sentence by sentence. It became a masterpiece of tactful pleading, a *kunstwerk* of rueful rebellion. It contained the case against Russian anti-Semitism in the most forceful yet respectful terms. The *rebs* looked at it and decided it was good.

By that time, poor Hannahle could see that her problem was taking a back seat. By mutual consent of everyone but her, she had been shelved. The one year she had resigned herself to waiting would become two, three, maybe forever. The mills of these gods had stopped grinding at all.

She went in despair to Elka. "Mother, what can I do now? What would you do?"

Elka thought. "If your father can do nothing with those old men, you certainly can't. You know how proud they are of him. People come from all around to ask his advice. But I tell you, Hannahle, if you can get the consent of the *rebs,* I have a hearing for you at the Russian school. I talked and talked to all my customers, and finally one of them went to the Direktor of the Russian school to tell him about you. The Direktor says you can come and apply to the school when they see all the new students. But the time is soon. Do something, or this is another chance you will miss. What I can do I am doing."

Hannah went in despair to Reb Israel. "Father, what can I

do? What are you doing to convince them? I must go to school this year. I can't wait."

Reb Israel thought. "It was better not to push before, Hannahle. The *rebs* could think of nothing but this petition. Until it was written there was no use asking them to decide anything else. Even yet it isn't finished. But come, *mein kind.* I will take you to *rebs.* Maybe you and I together can do what I can't do alone."

Hannah put her hand in her father's and took the walk she so often took with him to the *shul.* This time it was different. And what could she accomplish that her all-powerful, respected father had not? If anything, her coming to the *shul* to plead her case would make her seem presumptuous. What the wise men of the village decided was not to be changed by a very little girl.

Hand in hand the small man and the little girl entered the *shul,* and walked over to the long table where the *rebs* sat and argued and settled the community problems. Hannah was so tiny she could barely see over the top of the table.

The rebs were arguing about their *proshenya,* the petition to the Czar. Should the word they used be this or that? Reb Israel settled the discussion. No question about it, it should be that. Hannah listened. All at once she knew she would be going to the Russian school. The *rebs* might all be wise men, but perhaps they weren't as familiar with the fables of Krilov as she was. She knew very well the story of who would bell the cat. "Excuse me," she said, her voice loud and unafraid. Now that she knew how to plead her case, all her doubts had left her. "Is that your *proshenya* to the Czar?"

"*Sha,* Hannahle," her father said frowningly, "this is nothing for you. *Sha. Sha.*"

"Please, Father, please, all of you listen to me. Which one of you will write your *proshenya* to petition the Czar? Who is going to write the scroll?"

"Reb Chiam, of course," said her father. "You know his

Hebrew script is a work of art, something to make us all proud."

"And will the Czar read Reb Chiam's beautiful Hebrew script? Do you think the Czar knows Hebrew? Send me to school and I will learn to write your *proshenya* in Russian, in the very language of the Czar. Then maybe he'll read what you wise men are telling him."

Reb Israel covered his face with his hands. For the first time anyone could remember, the *reb* laughed in *shul*. "Hannahle, if you wanted to, like Queen Esther with King Ahasuerus, you would marry the Czar and save all our Jews. Well, wise *rebs* of the *shul,* does my daughter go to her school and learn how to write our *proshenya* in Russian? Or are we less wise than a six-year-old girl?"

The wise men were not at all stupid. One by one they agreed. Hannah could go to school.

Hannah and the Russians

NOW THAT HANNAH had official permission from the ghetto greats to go to Russian school, she had to let the Russians know they were going to receive her. Not only were paying Jews not welcome in the Russian school, but the recent intensification of anti-Semitism had made a sympathetic Direktor warn the school's Jews that "for their own good" they had better withdraw.

Elka talked seriously to Hannahle. "Darling, I know how much you want to go, and my customer has arranged your appointment for a new student examination, but don't you think you should wait? After all, another year . . . you won't be so old."

"No, Mother," said Hannahle, "I can't wait. Already I'll be a year older than anyone in the First Form. I should have gone last year. I can't put it off, not even a week, not even a minute. When is my examination?"

"The day after tomorrow. I didn't tell you because I am frightened. I don't think you should go."

"Never mind, Mother, Don't worry. But what will I do for my examination? I have nothing prepared and it's not much time."

"No, no *mein kind*. Would I let you go not prepared? All

year I have been preparing you in the store. You have done your examination over and over again. You will do it perfectly."

Hannah stared at Elka. It was the first time she ever really doubted her. Hannah knew very well she had been doing no lessons. "What will I do, Mother, that I have done over and over again?"

"You will tell one of the fables of Krilov. That is what they teach in the First Form. And when you tell it so perfectly, you will see, they will believe you belong in the Russian school. It's for that that Petrov has been making you recite again and again. And, of course, it makes the customers happy, too. That is the spoken part of the examination. For the written part, you will do arithmetic. No one can add kopeks faster than you. When you see the numbers written down, just pretend they are kopeks and you are making change in the store. You see"—Elka was proud—"you see, I have sent you to Russian school right here in the store."

"You're sure, Mother? Just to tell a fable is enough? But in the Russian school they teach you to be a scholar. It isn't just for storytelling!"

"I'm sure, Hannahle. Don't worry. If my little girl is going to school, she is going to show them all what we teach here in the ghetto."

Hannah wasn't really convinced. To her it seemed that the fables were too much fun to be proper schoolwork. But two days was no time at all in which to prepare anything. And anyway, what could she prepare? What Elka said was true. She could add kopeks faster than anyone, faster even than the *rebs* in the *shul*. Maybe she could get by on her arithmetic. If she had gotten this far, it seemed reasonable she would go all the way. She had learned early that once you've done your best and then a little more, that's all you can do.

The day after tomorrow came. Hannah walked the *viersts* to the Russian school. She was dressed in her best, which in-

cluded her Moscow cousin's outgrown shoes. That was something of a mistake because the rich Moscow cousin was three
years younger than Hannah, and her shoes were much too
small. Hannah's feet hurt.

Hannah was all alone. It was bad enough that she had to
make the long trip from the ghetto to school. No one else in
the family would. And, after all, no matter how good a head
Hannah had on her shoulders, she was only six, almost seven,
years old.

She went into the school and asked a man in her peasant
Russian, "Please, sir, where are the new student examinations?" His answer was unintelligible, but his finger pointed
up the stairs. She walked up, trembling. Suddenly she knew
that she could never qualify to go to school in this enormous
building with the big stairs.

At the top of the stairs there were long halls, one on each
side and one straight ahead. She went straight ahead until she
heard young voices. That must be the examination. There was
a heavy door in front of her. She pushed it open, but it would
not push. She pushed harder and harder, until finally, with a
running leap that took all her strength, it opened and she
found herself falling into a huge room, bigger than any she
had ever seen. There was a child up on the lecture platform,
reciting. And there were rows and rows of seats, filled with
other children waiting their turn for the examination.

Hannah walked as quietly as she could to the back of the
room. She sat down. Her feet hurt terribly, and as she heard
the other children reciting, her heart sank. They were telling
little poems, things she'd never heard, written by famous Russians. Recitation after recitation was given, and not one child
told a Krilov fable. It seemed Elka must have made a mistake.
Finally, after forty-two recitations, it was Hannah's turn.

She walked up to the platform, a tiny figure; half starved,
she was smaller than any of the fat and red-cheeked peasant

children. It seemed to her a very long walk. Her shoes hurt even more. She was frightened. The five men sitting in the front row, the Direktor and his assistants, seemed very big, very stern, and very *goyische* with their short hair and clean-shaven faces. She walked up the three steps and turned around.

"Pretend you are sitting on the table in the store and say your piece just the way you always do." That's what Elka had said when she left in the morning. She looked down. There were the five men, looking at her. She couldn't pretend they were customers in the store; they were too strange and too grand. Then she looked at the children. Well, a fable was a story for children. She would tell it to them.

She started her favoite, the story of the wolf and the crane. Almost as soon as she opened her mouth and started speaking her peasant Russian, the children were laughing. Hannah wouldn't be discouraged. She was telling these children a good story. Let them laugh. She would tell it to the end. She deepened her voice for the part of the wolf. She lilted it for the part of the crane. When she came to the climax, she forgot entirely where she was and yelled out the wolf's admonition in her loudest, gruffest voice: "Be off with you! Be off with you, and be sure you never cross my path again!" The children laughed and laughed. Hannah looked. The Direktor was laughing, too. Hannah walked off the platform, sadly. You did not laugh at a child you were going to let into the school. They hadn't laughed at any of the others.

It didn't matter that the written part of the examination was so easy—simply to write down the Russian alphabet that old Petrov had taught her to read and write in the store, and then to add some very simple sums. That she knew she could do. But her Russian was simply too bad. She hadn't learned it well enough; she hadn't worked hard enough; and she had been thinking about how much her feet ached.

She went home to Elka. "Mother, they laughed at me. They didn't like it. I failed and I'll never go to the Russian school."

"Who said that?" asked Elka. "I don't believe it. Did you do what I told you? Did you tell it just the way you do in the store?"

"Just the way you said, Mother. But they didn't like it."

"We'll see. We'll see. There's time enough to worry when you know you failed. But I don't believe a daughter of mine, and especially not my Hannahle, could fail an examination. After all, your father is Reb Israel."

Elka might not think much of her husband's practical common sense, but she knew that he was unmatched in academic achievement. And Hannah combined the two wisdoms— Elka's for getting things done, Reb Israel's for learning. How could she fail?

But Hannah knew what she knew. She stopped thinking of the Russian school altogether. And she had nothing else to think of. She went into an alarming decline. She wouldn't recite in the store; the very name of Krilov made her shudder, and she burst into tears when someone said, "Hannahle, do the wolf story again."

Then there came a letter to the ghetto. That in itself was an event, because most of the correspondence was sent through the *shul*. When a traveler was going from Borschevka to somewhere else, he took the mail with him and dropped it off at another *shul*, until it got where it was going. Very few people used the post. Stamps cost real money. The letter was addressed to Hannah. Reb Israel came running: "Hannahle, Hannahle, you've received a letter, a real letter through the post. The school must have accepted you. Come, Hannahle, I'm going to open it." The whole family stood around while Reb Israel opened the letter. Painfully, Hannahle read it out. "This is to inform you that you will report to the Third Form, Room 7, on

October one. Please come with a notebook, a clean handkerchief, and your Jew tuition."

"Hannahle, you've read it wrong. It must be the First Form.
You are only six, not even seven yet."

"No, Father. We can bring it to Petrov, but it says, absolutely, Third Form."

"You see, Israel," said Elka, "I told you she could not have
failed. She passed so well they are putting her two years ahead.
My customer told me they do that sometimes with remarkable
students. He said Hannahle shouldn't worry about missing
last year. But of course her, you can't tell *her* anything. She
knows that if they laugh at you they won't pass you."

Elka picked up her tiny *wunder* and danced and danced
around the room, laughing and laughing and laughing at her
while the rest stood and clapped.

Reb Israel stopped them. "And what about the Jew tuition?
I told you, Hannahle, I can't give you a kopek."

"That's all right, Father. I promised you won't have to pay.
You won't have to pay, and I won't go to school on *Shabbus*.
And the peasants won't come near me. I'm going to school;
I'm really going to school."

Hannah had to go again to the Russian school, but this time
it didn't look nearly so frightening—just a big building
where they were going to teach her so many things that there
were to know. She went up to the guard at the door, not such a
big man now, with plenty of time to answer a little girl's questions.

"Please, sir, I have a letter. I must talk to the Direktor."
Again, she could not understand what he said through his
bristly moustache, but she followed his pointing finger.

Written right on the door she saw the words "Direktor,"
and next to it, "Sokolov." She held her letter tight in her hand,
and knocked. Her hand was brave, even if she was just a little
less so, now.

"Come in."

She walked into an office that seemed to her magnificent, lined as it was with so many books, more books than she knew there were.

"Please, sir, the Direktor," she said, and he still looked as big as he ever had. "I have a letter. I have to talk to you."

She handed him the letter, and waited. "Yes?" he said. "But this is very clear. You are to report to Third Form on October one. This isn't even September. What are you doing here?"

"Well, it says I must report with a notebook, a clean handkerchief, and my Jew tuition. But I must tell you now, I will not be able to pay. We have no money for school."

"I see," said the Direktor. "Why did you apply without telling us you couldn't pay?"

"I thought I had to do one thing at a time. The first thing I had to do was get admitted to Russian school."

"And why did you want to come to Russian school at all?"

"Because I am living in Russia, not in a Jewish country. I should go to the Russian school."

"You may be right, you may be right; I hope you are the future. You're the little girl, aren't you, who told the story of the wolf and the crane? You told it very well."

"But everyone laughed. I thought they didn't like it."

"Yes, of course everyone laughed. But they loved it. I loved it. Don't worry, Hannah Kleegman; you can come to my school on scholarship. You don't have to pay any Jew tuition."

"Thank you very much, but please, sir, the Direktor."

"Yes," said Sokolov.

"You know my father is Reb Israel Kleegman, a very important man in our *shul,* a very pious man, too."

"Yes," said Sokolov.

"Well, I had to make him a promise so that he would let me come to the Russian school."

"Yes," said Sokolov.

"I promised him I would not come to classes on Saturday,

because Saturday is our *Shabbus,* Sabbath, and it is a sin for me. If I work very hard the rest of the week, and do all my exercises and all my lessons and all my extra work at home on Sunday, do you think it will be all right?"

"Yes," said Sokolov. "Now, Hannah Kleegman, tell me, are you saving anything else that you must do or can't do or should do? Is there any other way you plan to change things in my school?"

"No, sir, the Direktor."

"Good," said Sokolov. "Then we have an agreement. You can bring a notebook and a clean handkerchief with you October one, can't you?"

"Oh, yes, sir," said Hannah.

"And you will come, since it is not a Saturday."

"Oh, yes, sir," said Hannah.

"Good-bye, Hannah Kleegman. It is my pleasure to have met you."

And he sent Hannah home without her having any idea how remarkable this interview had been. After all, she had always known she could convince the Russians if she could convince the *rebs.*

Once Hannah started school, she discovered that she was learning more than lessons in the Russian school; she was learning a moneymaking trade. Now her Russian was school Russian, not the peasant Russian of the unlettered.

From her first week, she began passing on her lessons to the children of the wealthier Jews in the Borschevka ghetto. As she learned, she taught.

And her own adventuring blazed a trail for others. Before Hannah, no Jewish child of Borschevka had thought of going to the Russian school. Once she started there, and then started giving lessons, many of the better-off Jews began thinking of sending their children. After all, if Reb Israel Ketointe's daughter could go, it couldn't be an impious thing; it must be a good thing. Slowly but surely the children of the ghetto would be sent out of it. And in the years left before the Revolution, young Borschevkans prepared themselves to live in a Russian world. It soon became one of the accepted events of the ghetto that each month Hannahle would come home from school, the last day of the month, and call her pupils around her. "See what you get when you work hard? Honor!" And she showed her certificate of honor, proof that once again she was first in her class.

Hannah Goes to School

Once Hannah reported for her first class on October one, with a clean handerchief and a notebook and no tuition, she discovered how right she had been, Hannah was made for school. While the others scratched their heads over the problems set them, Hannah raced through. Even when she was set extra work she seemed to be finished well ahead of the others. She had plenty of time to look around her, and observe. And lots of time to catch up on the few things the others had learned in the first two years, that she did not know.

Tiny as she was, and two years younger than any of the other students, she had to become a teacher's pet. And her wise teacher managed to keep her away from the teasing and harassing of the other peasant children by giving her extra instruction for the first two months during her recess periods.

Soon, however, she was accepted as a kind of class mascot, a little "freak" who always knew the answer and who could be depended upon to help an older student who couldn't get the hang of his homework.

"Hannah, come here and help me."

"Hannah, how do you do this?"

These came to be the most common cries heard in the free

class periods. The teacher stopped interfering, and let Hannah make her own place in the classroom.

Among the children she had one good friend and worthy rival. He was the mayor's son, and therefore not one of the rude peasant boys her father had made her promise to stay away from.

A very bright boy, also old beyond his years, he felt fatherly and protective toward little Hannah. The two of them were the only scholars in the class. Together they could answer every question, never making a mistake. They were destined to tie for first certificate throughout their school careers. Together, each of them took home each month the certificate of honor that meant leadership in the class.

But Ivan was much more worldly-wise than Hannah, and understood how much she needed protecting. Many of the boys and girls in the Third Form were teen-agers who had started their schooling late or who would never go any higher in school.

These were earthy boys and girls who would leave school to marry, out of inclination, out of necessity. The recess hours were already being spent in the exploration of pleasures that marriage might hold out for them.

Hannah, always a quick observer, was somewhat puzzled. "Ivan," she said one day, "Ivan, what does Petrov look for in Marousia's blouse? In fact, why are the big boys always putting their hands down the front of the girls' blouses? What are they looking for there?"

"Why, Hannah," said Ivan, desperately looking for a way to protect her innocence, "don't you know? The girls carry little apples in their blouses. That's what the boys are looking for. You know how much they like apples."

And since apples were a staple of every lunch hour at the school, Hannah was perfectly satisfied with this explanation.

Still, as time went on and they all got older, Ivan, no matter how he protected her, could not shield Hannah from the casual cruelty of the peasant children. Anti-Semitism was so much a part of their lives, it didn't even occur to them that they were being cruel to Hannah, whom most of them liked, when they came to school with the latest anti-Jewish slogans on their lips.

In her years of Russian school, anti-Semitism became worse and worse. Pogrom after pogrom was organized with the blessings of the Czar. A child would come to school and tell the assembled class, "My father really gave it to those lousy Jews in ———— last night." And Hannah would bring back to the ghetto the news of another attack, another pogrom. Often it was the first news that the isolated ghetto town had had.

During this time Hannah began to share Elka's dream. They would all, somehow, get to Amerika. It was not enough to leave the ghetto. For Jews, Russia was one big ghetto. And education was not enough. She was being educated. So were the peasant children in her class. Yet that education did nothing to change their attitude toward Jews. And neither did the fact that they all liked Hannah. She had thought a lot of the anti-Semitism around her arose from the Jews' determination to stay within the ghetto. Now she saw that the *rebs,* after all, knew something. While they stayed in the ghetto, at least they weren't inviting attack. No, coming out of Borschevka was not enough. Elka was right: they had to leave, to go where anyone could get ahead on his own merits, and where at least you could be free from government-directed pogroms. The Russian school was not, after all, a destination. It was only a stop along the way.

For the first time, Hannah, too, began to join in when Elka began her daily chant. Now as Elka said, "When we get to Amerika . . . in Amerika . . . it's not like that in Amerika," Hannah would say, "Father, what do you think? Isn't it much better to live in a free land? What kind of country is it where a Jew can live anywhere? In Amerika I could go to the university." It was a chant that grew in strength and persuasiveness as things got worse and worse around Borschevka. Soon, even Reb Israel was beginning to take up the chant. Occasionally, when Hannah became particularly bitter about something she had heard in school, he would comfort her with, "*Sha*, Hannahle, *sha*. In Amerika it won't be like this."

And Hannah, who in some ways understood things even better than Elka, began to change the tone of the chant. It wasn't "When we get to Amerika" that you heard from her, it was "When will we go to America? How soon can we save up the deposit? How will we manage?"

Her persistence was enough so that the family's vague plans began to take a certain form. Projects were suggested and abandoned. Letters were written and received. Real letters, by post to and from Amerika, a long, expensive way. They knew at least how others had tried and how they were doing. The Weismanns wrote and said Yes, it was true. America was a great land, a beautiful land. Work was there, waiting for people who were willing to work hard. Education was there, waiting for people who were willing to study hard. Their own Herschel was going to high school, a school like the Russian gymnasium. It cost nothing, and his teacher said he might even be able to go to the free college. And there were many girls in Herschel's class. It was true what Elka said, in Amerika the girls became professors and taught in the free schools.

Elka's dream became less and less just a dream. Russia was getting worse and worse. Rumors had it that a terrible pogrom was being planned right for their district. Borschevka, which had so far been too small to attract the worst, might become the center of a new wave of persecution. Something had to be done. So something was done. Meriam, the eldest daughter, would be sent over first. She would go to work and start paying on the ticket for Rachel. Then the two of them would work to earn enough money to start paying on tickets for the rest of the family. It was five dollars down and a dollar a week forever to pay off your ticket. And yet tickets were paid off; families did come.

Hannah wanted to go, too, but both Elka and Reb Israel said, "No." Reb Israel continued: "You do well here. You are learning much in the Russian school. Once you go to Amerika and start to work, no one knows if you will go back to school. You are our scholar. Your work is study. Do it and make us proud."

So Meriam was to go off to the unknown, fabled, unbelievable land. She would leave her fiancé, the son of a rabbi in the neighboring town, and go to Amerika. The trip was beginning. But immediately the rumors started. The town whispered about Reb Israel's oldest daughter who was recently engaged and now was being sent to Amerika. There was only one reason why a newly engaged girl was ever sent away on a long journey. Such a *shunde* in the family of Reb Israel! Reb Israel had to hear such a rumor only once. Meriam could not go to Amerika, and that was final. Not for another year. No one would say that he had sent away a pregnant daughter! But Elka was not to be put off for another year. If Meriam couldn't go, then Rachel would start and Meriam would follow. What did it matter that Rachel was only fourteen? That was old enough. She could live with Tante Becky, and help out. Rachel was willing. She was not only willing; she was delighted. Never the most favored of the girls, still deaf from the aftereffects of the Borschevka pogrom, she was finally getting her chance, and what a chance! She would work for eight dollars a week, and she could keep out three dollars of that for herself. Surely three dollars was a vast sum to live on, but the family insisted she must live well. So Rachel went off alone. Fourteen. To start the family in Amerika. The trip was begun. Where one went, others must. And they all began saying: "We will leave for Amerika in three years, two years, one year. Rachel has left; Meriam will leave next year." No, it wasn't a dream at all anymore. It was with them as it was with so many . . . from a dream to a plan, to days that were measured in dollars sent.

Elka and Chiam had started it all. Elka and Israel would

live it. But the immenseness of it. The power of the dream. It had moved a tightly knit family with deep roots in a small provincial community to abandon two of their children to the vast unknown that was Amerika. It would move the rest of them away from everything that was familiar in their lives. And what moved them? After all, they wrote to people who lived in Amerika. Those people were still working as hard as it is possible to work to eke out a bare living. They even lived in slums and in ghettos. Many of them suffered a loneliness and isolation they had never known in Europe. And nobody lied about the bad things. They wrote home the truth as they lived it. But in the immigrants' letters certain things were taken for granted. Things about school, about the life of the poor, about the spirit of the new-country ghettos. When someone wrote complaining about working conditions, he forgot he was writing to families that could nowhere find any work. When another said he had lived on one meal a day for a whole month, he was complaining to a family who were lucky to have in a week what he ate for that one meal. But material goods were not enough to move them to the golden land. It was the spirit of the letters; it was the very complaints. When had it ever occurred to a Borschevkan to complain that things were bad? In Borschevka that was the way things were. Bad.

Hannah and the Doctor March

IT WAS WHEN she was eight, during the Russo-Japanese War, that Hannah had her first taste of doctoring, and such a terrible taste it was that it changed the whole life in front of her. She had shared Elka's ambition for her children. Hannah wanted to teach. What better thing could there be to do than to pass on her hard-won knowledge? To find others who burned as she did to learn, and then learn more and more and more. But she discovered there was something better, more important.

And this is how she learned. From all the towns around, the Czar's recruiters came and took the men off to fight a war with Japan. Japan? What kind of country was that? So far away, so small, and so many men had to go. The men left. Russian peasants, Jewish boys, off they went to fight. To fight who with what? The raw recruits wouldn't know one end of a gun from another. They weren't hunters or killers. They were farmers who trapped predators with cunning and patience, not with guns.

And off went the boys; many never were heard from again. But after a while, some of them came home. One, two at a time.

On one leg or even none. They had been discharged from the Czar's army. They were free, and why? Ah, they were wounded, wounded too badly to be patched up at an army medical station and sent back to fight. So what did the Czar's doctors do with them? They didn't even begin to patch them up. They discharged them right at the battlefield and left them to make their own way home. Of course, the ones with the worst wounds never made it, but some of the others did, limping, bleeding, begging their way across Russia to get themselves home. And when they got home, what help could they get? In Borschevka the local doctor came one day a month for three hours to a clinic in the town hall.

He treated everyone he could in that time. But that included the old and dying, the young and about to be born, the chronic patients who lived from month to month for the visit to the doctor. What can such a doctor do for an amputee who needed patient retraining, for an emergency case who arrived home almost with his last breath? Nothing. And he didn't want to do anything, either. The doctor said soldiers were the army's responsibility. Borschevka paid him only to care for his regular patients.

Time after time, a desperate wife, a despairing mother would come to Elka to beg a special herb or magic medicine to heal a wound. And what was there for her to give them? Some healing grasses, a clean bandage, a salve. Little armor against the gangrene that was claiming more lives around Borschevka than bullets had.

Elka shook her head and gave what she could. She always had a special feeling for the sick and the maimed. And a special feeling about what to do for them.

One day a particularly large number of remedies had been called for. The stories of wives and mothers had been especially sad. Elka just couldn't stand it. She closed the store, something she usually did only to have children or to observe the Sabbath.

"Hannahle," she called, "Hannahle, come here. We are going for a long walk. You will come with me and carry my basket. If all these women are coming to me in Borschevka, there must be many wounded soldiers in the countryside whose women can't come to town. We will go, you and I, and see what can be done. Nothing, nothing, of course. But we will try."

"Yes, Mother. What should I do?" Hannah was always eager to go.

"Can you still wear those shoes the rich cousin sent us?" said Elka.

"No, Mother, I can't even put them on."

"Well, first go find some sacks you can wrap around your feet. It will be a very long, very hard walk."

Elka made preparations, too. She went to her cupboards and looked them over. There, put away carefully, was the dress she had worn for her wedding, with its voluminous petticoats. She pulled down the box and took out petticoat after petticoat. There, put away very carefully, were her best linens, the sheets and cloths that had always been too good to use. Yellowed now, but still so beautifully stitched by the young Elka who was going to marry Chiam, by the young Elka who sewed with her dreams.

This was no time for dreams. Men were dying out of simple neglect, because nobody cared. If Elka didn't care enough to give a few rags, what good was she?

"Hannah, come here."

"Yes, Mother."

"You tear. You tear first."

"But, Mother, all your beautiful things."

"Hannah, you learn to be the strong one for all of us. Tear."

And she and Hannah worked together for three days, cutting and tearing the linens and petticoats into rags. The material was so strong it fought back at them, resisting the change from beauty into bandages. Finally, they had a basket full of bandages. Bandages? They were clean rags in long strips. But they would do.

Another two days Hannah and Elka went into the fields. They gathered plants and grasses, flowers and seeds—the special healers of the poor. And from them Elka made a healing salve, something she had created in the store to soften the nipples of nursing mothers when they cracked. It soothed and cured. It was all Elka had to offer.

They wrapped their feet in the sacks. They planned to make a big circuit around Borschevka. They might walk as far as a hundred miles. There would be mud and stones and hard, hard road to walk for the two of them. They wore rags; they carried rags. What mercy did they bring with them?

First they stopped into the homes of the nearby soldiers, the men whose wives and mothers had been to the store. Elka examined the wounds, and realized she would have to go back. What use was healing salve applied on top of filth? So, to her precious store of soap she went and put it all in the basket. First she would wash; then she would heal. They set out again. Even though it wasn't winter, there was a chill in the air and the ground was cold under their feet.

The two left town carrying their baskets. Neither of them thought of it as an errand of mercy. It was something that had to be done. It seemed only they would do it. They talked as they walked, not of what they were doing or where they were going, but always of the dream, the same dream, the only dream. Amerika. And if it seemed very far away to Hannah, still it was something to talk about as they walked.

They came to the next town. Here, still, they were treating soldiers whose wives had begged remedies of Elka. Here it was just a question of cleaning and continuing the treatment. The wives talked to Elka as though she were the doctor himself. She did what she could. She pretended it would help.

And when she got to the next town she saw how much it really did help, because here, for the first time, were soldiers who had never used Elka's soothing salves or healing herbs.

At the first house, she stopped and told them why she was here and what she could do.

"We have no one wounded here, but go two houses down. They need you, and God bless you."

And two houses down was a man whose arm had received a blast of shrapnel. Elka went to work. She said nothing as she worked and worked, while a wide-eyed Hannah stared unbelievingly at the tortured flesh. Finally, it was bandaged and out of sight. They left with the thanks and blessings of the house on their heads.

"Mother, you can't help that man. He must have the doctor. Why isn't there a doctor?" Hannah barely waited until she was out of the house before she burst out indignantly. Then she stopped speaking, and was sick.

"There's no doctor because he is a poor man, a peasant. Who cares what happens to him? Who will listen if you tell them he is going to die? And from that wound of course he'll die. Soon."

"But somebody must care. He's a Russian. I know the Russians don't care about Jews, but don't they care about Russians?"

"About the poor, nobody cares."

They walked on and on. At night they were taken into the last house they had visited. At mealtime the people shared what little food there was in the house. Time after time Elka treated a wound that there was no healing.

Hannah stopped being sick, but she despaired.

"What good does it do, Mother, for us to walk farther and farther? You aren't even helping them and you are wearing yourself out."

"No, Hannah, never believe that. It helps that someone comes. It helps that I do clean the wounds. Even, I see, it helps to give them my salves and herbs. The wounds that have had something on them are better than the ones that have never been treated. Anyway, even if it doesn't help one soldier, it helps me and it should help you."

"Why, Mother, why should it help if you can't heal?"

"Because you are doing something. The world is filled with people who do nothing, who let terrible things happen and are only glad it isn't happening to them. That's no way to live in the world. You must behave as though everything you do is important; then it will be."

Hannah didn't agree. Elka was exhausting all her energy on this trip. How could Hannah tell her it was useless? How could she make Elka believe it?

Many times they came too late to do anything at all. The soldier was already dead. Yet the family seemed comforted that finally someone had come. Elka knew what to say, and Hannah listened.

One wound merged in Hannah's mind into another, one bandaging into another, one meal, one night, one stay into another. And then finally it was over. There were no more bandages in the basket. The salves and herbs had all been given away. It was time to go home, the march was over, the march to the wounded soldiers, the doctor march.

The two turned back. There weren't even rags on their feet anymore, but their baskets were light and empty. As they walked through the towns, people came out and waved. And after the two went a wave of sound, a rising whisper. In Russian, in Malarussian, in Yiddish the words of blessing followed them, the words of recognition: "There goes Elka and her daughter Hannah. God bless you, God keep you."

And Hannah understood something new, something she hadn't learned from all the doctoring, all the walking, or even all of Elka's talking.

"Mother, when we go to Amerika, I won't be a teacher; all a teacher can do is tell people things—wonderful things and important things. But you are right it isn't enough to tell people. You must do. People only really understand what you do.

There are not enough doctors in Russia for the people. I will learn to be a doctor, and then I will come back here and treat the peasants."

And, at eight, unlikely as it seemed when she walked through Russia, she had made up her mind—a mind that never left a goal once it was fixed. Hannah had started her medical education.

Meanwhile, Back at the School . . .

MEANWHILE things for Hannah were good. She was doing very well in the Russian school. She and Ivan were fast friends. Together they dreamed other dreams—not dreams of a future together—but dreamed together of each other's future.

Hannah would say: "Ivan, someday when you are Mayor of Borschevka, like your father, maybe I'll come back to visit. And I will come to you in your mayor's office, where you will be very fat and so important. Of course you will wear your chain and badge. You will greet me, a distinguished foreigner from Amerika, and you will say, 'Welcome, welcome, distinguished madame, to Borschevka; let me show you around my little village.' And then I'll say to you: 'Silly, Ivan, it's Hannahle; don't you remember when we went walking on the meadow together?' And then how we'll laugh."

"Oh, no," Ivan would say, "it won't be like that at all. I will come to Amerika on a visit. And I'll become terribly sick. And no one will know what is wrong with me. And I'll be lying there waiting to die because I am so sick, and in will come the famous doctor, Hannah Kleegman, called by the ambassador because she is the only one who can help me. And you'll come

and look at me and say, 'It's obvious, he has blublublublu-
philcolis. I will operate at once?' And you'll operate, and when
I open my eyes you'll be standing there, and I'll say, 'Aren't
you Hannah Kleegman?' and you'll say, 'Yes,' and I'll say, 'But
I'm Ivan!' And then how happy we'll be to see each other!"

And together they would dream separate dreams of a life
neither could share in reality. Marvelous dreams that made
their friendship stronger. There were many good years together—six in all from those first months when he be-
friended her. But then they had to face a conflict. It would
soon be time to graduate. Even though the school had been
giving each of them Number One Honor Certificates every
month, there could be only one real Number One Diploma
from the school. Someone had to be first. With two pupils who
had yet to make a single mistake in the work, who had always
gotten 100 percent on the examinations, what were they to do?
Who could decide who would get the Number One Diploma?
This was a thing of real importance. There had to be a best.
For weeks they discussed it between themselves as a problem.
Then the teacher called them in. That was good. After all, at
twelve, this was too hard a problem for Hannah.

"Hannah and Ivan," the teacher said, "you are both excellent students, two of the best I've ever had. In any other year
since I've been teaching, either one of you would have been
outstanding, unquestionably Number One. This year we
must pick between the two of you, so there will be a special
examination that only you two will take. It will be a hard
examination. And whoever gets the best mark will be our
Number One student, the holder of the Number One Diploma. However, I want you to remember that, as far as I am
concerned, you are both Number One students."

It was the kindest thing a teacher had ever said to either of
them. Both children were relieved. The problem of who was
really Number One was going to be solved.

The day of the hard examination came. Both students had

studied conscientiously. Both were trying very hard. In a way their friendship made each of them a little more determined to win the Number One Diploma away from the other. They were given their hard examination papers. Hannah looked at hers, and smiled. It was a little harder than the regular exams, but it was all work she knew very well. She answered question after question easily. If the teachers at the Russian school really thought this was hard, they should hear some of the questions the *rebs* at the *shul* used to ask. That was argument and philosophy. That was hard. But this was only facts. And facts were things you knew if you had studied them. Particularly if you were like Hannah and had only to close your eyes to see a whole page in front of you with all the writing on it. Sometimes she would play that trick for Father, because he enjoyed it so. She would look at the open prayer book; then he would take it from her and say, "Hannah, read me the fourth line from the bottom on the right-hand side."

And she would begin reading, going on and on until the delighted Reb Israel said: "*Schon,* Hannahle. That's enough. You will tire your mind."

So she answered all the questions on the examination. It was a long, long paper. But she was finished before the time was up. Only after she had handed her paper in did she look at Ivan. And he was signing his paper, too, and handing it in.

They left together. "It wasn't really hard," said Ivan. "No, not really," said Hannah. "We've got extra time. Shall we go to the top of the hill before we go home?"

"Yes," said Ivan. "Come on, let's run." And, since that was one of the things they liked to do best together, they ran up and down the hill, winding up in a giggling roll that sent them bumping together and left them at the bottom, dizzy and breathless.

Again they were called to come together to see their teacher. "I'm afraid my plan didn't work," he said, looking at them sternly. "You both got a hundred on the test. So, we will try once again. This time it will be a much harder test. We must find someone to win the Number One Diploma."

The two children looked at each other. It had been too simple. Things never were that simple. In the world they lived in, people never were able to say This is how it is and That is how it was. From the beginning it had been clear to them that between them there was no Number One. They would just take longer examination after longer examination, but none would really be the end. Only they could decide how it would be.

They went out together. Ivan held out his hand; Hannah took it.

"To the top of the hill?" he asked.

"To the top of the hill," she answered.

"All right, Hannah, what are we going to do?" Ivan asked the question as he surveyed the town down below them. "We must find some way to give one of us the diploma."

"You are the boy," said Hannah tentatively. "Is it more important to you?"

"No," said Ivan, "you are going to be a great doctor. And you are a girl and a Jew. It is just as important to you. Maybe more. But that is no fair way to decide. We must discover who is best."

"Best at what? At examinations? Neither of us is. There is no best between us."

"Oh, there is best. I'm the best spitter. You can't spit at all. I'm the best hitter. You are the best reader and the best talker. You can speak four languages already: German, Russian, Yiddish, and Hebrew. All I speak is Russian. There is best. But at certificates how do we find it?"

"What else do we do just as well as each other?"

"I don't really know, or maybe, who is the best runner?"

"Sometimes you, sometimes me. But at least it isn't always a tie."

"Then," said Ivan firmly, "that's how we decide. We will run a race. If you win, I will miss two questions on the examination. If I win, you will. Is it fair?"

"Yes."

"Is it agreed?"

"Yes."

"Now?"

"Now."

They stood together, hands interlocked, and looked down from the top of the hill. Then they looked at each other. They were on a level, eye looking into eye. Perhaps never again could they be so equal, so much in agreement about the world. The mayor's son, the ghetto girl who saw together a future they could not share. As they stood together on the hill, what they saw were the marvelous possibilities, each for the other.

Their hands separated. He gave the starting signal. They ran. At the bottom of the hill Hannah was ahead. She ran past the old tree that was always the end of their races. And she had won. She turned quickly. "Ivan, maybe it's not fair."

"No, Hannah. It was agreed. It was fair. You are the Diploma Number One."

"Maybe I will miss questions, too."

"Ah, Hannah, that's just why I said the loser must make two mistakes. Possibly, we could both make one. Two makes it certain. If you make two mistakes, too, I will know that you have not behaved with honor. Remember, to a man honor is most important. You must stay with our agreement. You must do your best. Anyway, Hannah, you could never do anything else."

"Nothing else. Nothing less. You know, Ivan, if I had lost, how could I have missed two questions? I tell you, it wasn't fair."

"You know why it is fair, Hannah? Because you have lost many races to me. But when it was a race for the Diploma Number One, you did not lose. You could not lose. You had to win. And when you must, you will always win. In that way, I am not as strong as you. Maybe I *am* as bright. But I would not, perhaps, have made my way out of the ghetto. Come on, Hannah, we've decided, it's a marvelous day. What shall we do with the rest of it? Come on, Hannah, let's *run.*"

And, once again, he took her hand, and they ran together till neither could draw a breath without whooping from the deep pain of breathing inside them.

The day of the next examination gave them no problems. They came to it happily. The decision had been made. They were both satisfied. Ivan handed his paper in with two questions answered wrong. He finished before Hannah. He smiled at her as he left.

When she signed her paper and walked out, he was waiting for her.

"Hello, Diploma Number One," he greeted her.

"It was a long, hard examination, this time," she said.

"Yes, but was there any question on it that you didn't know?"

"No," said Hannah.

"Or me," said Ivan.

The next summons was from the Direktor. And it was for Hannah, alone.

"Hannah Kleegman," said the Direktor. "We have a serious problem."

"I'm sorry. Have I done something wrong?" Hannah asked.

"No. Maybe the world has, but not you, Hannah Kleegman," said the Direktor. "All you have done is win the Number One Diploma. But that is a serious problem. You know all the diplomas must be signed first by me and then by the priest. Well, the priest refuses to sign your diploma. He says he will not certify a Jew as the best student in the class. He says it is not holy to do so, and not even Russian to do so. He will not sign your diploma."

"Can I have an unsigned diploma?"

"Oh, I will sign it. I will sign it twice. But you must go

much further on with your schooling. You are not going to
stop here, at this village school. And they won't accept your
credentials if the diploma is not signed properly."

"Well, what should I do? Why are you telling me this?"

"I don't know myself, why I bother to tell you. If I can't do
anything, why do I think you can? The priest will not sign.
That's all. And if you go on to the gymnasium, they will not
credit your diploma. Perhaps if you are willing to take Diploma Number Three or Four, I can get the priest to sign. But
it will amount to the same thing. If you are not the best, you
can't hope to get into another school. No, it is no use."

"No, I will not take a lower diploma. It wouldn't be honorable. And I have promised to be honorable."

"And what is so honorable about the whole thing? It is a
shame, a great shame, but what can I do?"

The Direktor looked at her, consideringly. "You know,
Hannah Kleegman, there is something I can do. I have hesi-
tated to even mention it, but now, maybe, is the time. Do not
be angry with me. I know how proud you are of your father,
but think before you answer me. I can get the priest to sign
your Number One Diploma. And I can guarantee your education. Not just in this school and the gymnasium. But all the
way until you do become a doctor. You have to do only one
thing. And you don't have to do that with your heart, only
your head, that head that is so quick at your studies. I hope it is
as quick to grab an opportunity."

"What should I do?" asked Hannah. She listened quietly.

"Join the church. Convert. Once you are no longer Jewish,
I can do everything for you. Arrange for scholarships, and I
myself will pay all your other expenses. Think, Hannah
Kleegman; you can have what you want so much. And it
doesn't have to be a big thing. Who will know what prayers
you say?"

"God will know. My father will know. I will know. I will
take the diploma signed by you. In Amerika it will serve."

As she left, Ivan met her just outside the door of the school.

"Well, now you have the diploma?"

"Yes and no. I have it, but the priest will not sign it, so it will not help me to get into a gymnasium."

"That is no good to you at all. Why won't the priest sign it?"

"Because it is wrong for a Jew to win Diploma Number One."

"That is no good at all, either. I will talk to my father."

What Ivan told his father he did not tell Hannah, but what happened became Borschevka history.

Ivan came to Hannah two days later. "It is all fixed. You have a good Number One Diploma. It will get you into the gymnasium or into a school anywhere. It is all signed."

"But the priest said he would never sign it."

"He didn't."

"Then how can it be good?"

"My father signed it."

"Your father—but why would he sign my diploma?"

"Because I told him it was a question of honor. After all, if you didn't get the real Number One Diploma, I would. And it would be a dishonor for me. My father could not allow that."

So, Hannah Kleegman had the first Borschevka lower-school diploma signed by the mayor.

It seemed very important at the time, but in the end it didn't really matter. The three years were finally up, and Reb Israel was taking his family to Amerika. In Amerika, who would ever have heard of the Mayor of Borschevka?

The Kleegmans Take the Boat

MERIAM AND RACHEL were already in Amerika. In four years they had paid enough on the passage to bring the whole family over. There were Reb Israel, Elka, Hannah, and the new baby, Sophie—whom Elka had produced, like some God-inspired Sarah, in her fiftieth year. The four of them had said their good-byes, and been blessed by the family they left behind. Reb Israel's brother had taken Hannah aside and given her a special blessing.

"Go always in the sight of God, my daughter, and never forget you are a good girl and a good Jew."

"How could I forget I am a Jew, Uncle?"

"But, Hannah, that's one of the miracles of America. In America it is possible to forget you are a Jew."

Ivan had come to say good-bye, entering into the ghetto, something he had never done before.

"Remember, Hannah, remember the hill and the Number One Diploma and our race. And remember, you will be a famous doctor. I will come to Amerika to see you. I will try."

They made no promises to write each other. Always they had been honest with each other. Even now, when it was hardest, they were honest that it was good-bye. Reb Israel watched Ivan leave. He gave him the accolade a good Jew never gives a *shagetz,* a Christian man, visiting his daughter. *"A shaine yunge mann."* A beautiful young man, the Jewish mark of approval.

The family found they had few belongings they wanted to take to the new world. Reb Israel's own writings and commentaries. Those had to come. His prayer shawls and phylacteries. Those had to come. Elka and Hannah had so few clothes, they would wear most of what they owned. Furniture? So worn, so heavy—why bring it anywhere? Pots and pans? In the end they showed their real faith in Amerika, where everything would be better. They left almost everything behind.

But what they had had to be all packed, not to go to Amerika, but to go to visit the great rabbi in Austria. The rabbi was Reb Israel's idol, the man to whom he turned for reassurance of the goodness of God and the validity of the Talmud. As the *rebs* of Borschevka felt that Reb Israel Ketointe was the final authority on anything, Reb Israel, during a lifetime of correspondence, had come to regard the great rabbi as the surrogate of the Almighty Himself.

The great rabbi lived in a small Austrian ghetto, where his home was a way station for every wandering and wondering Jew who stopped to feast on his crumbs of wisdom. Austria was on the way to Amerika. So everything was packed up, bundled in, and the Kleegman family began its hegira by wagon, by walking, by train. It was fully understood that the journey was to ask the advice of the great rabbi. If he said No, there would be no Amerika. If he said Yes, the journey was really begun.

The Kleegmans arrived by train on a Friday in the winter of 1906. That meant that they must make at least a two-day stay. It was *Shabbus by nacht,* the eve of the Sabbath, and no work, no advice, no conferences could be held until after sundown on Saturday. The huge table was set for the Sabbath feast. Around it sat the Hasidim, the orthodox Jewish men who

were simply unable to take a holiday from arguing the eso-
terica of law and ritual; and the four Kleegmans. Reb Israel,
who found at last his peers in propounding the enigmas of the
Lord; Elka, who knew only one thing—the great rabbi had to
speed them on their way, anything else was unthinkable;
Sophia—too small to do anything but lie in her mother's
arms, as the weight of uncertainty lay on Elka's heart; and
Hannah, who took one stand, never to leave her father, so that
she could be sure of what the great rabbi was going to say to
him and change it in some way if it wasn't right.

One thing was clear to the Kleegman women. If Reb Israel
spent very long in this stimulating atmosphere of constant
argument and debate, it would be impossible to move him.
They would have exchanged their own ghetto for a foreign
one, that offered even less.

At last the time came. The great rabbi would see Reb Israel
and advise him. Reb Israel told the great rabbi how first
Rachel, then Meriam, had gone to America, and now they had
paid the deposit for the rest of the family to come. Was it the
will of God that the Kleegmans should leave Europe? Or
should Reb Israel stay to offer help and comfort in the bleak
times coming to Borschevka? Should he give up his position,
the respect of his townspeople, the way of life he had been
born to, to start again in a world that was as new as it was un-
predictable? Did a pious man do well to carry God's wisdom
where it did not seem nearly as important as it did in Borschevka? And could he, at his age, make the change to new customs, new people, a new life?

Hannah listened in amazement. It was as though her father
now lived in Paradise and were leaving it. She had always
thought of the trip from Borschevka to Amerika as a flight into the Garden of Eden.

But the great rabbi understood perfectly what Reb Israel
was saying. And he answered gravely:

"Reb Israel, consider. What are you leaving? The respect of

your fellowmen, your neighbors? Wherever you go your learning will command respect. The ability to help others? Nowhere will you find a place where others do not need help. Nowhere, not even in Paradise, for it couldn't be Paradise if one could not do good there. In Amerika you have two lovely daughters who have worked hard to bring you to them. Go to the *goldene medina,* the golden land, and bring your family together once again."

So Austria became the first stop on their way.

From Austria, they had to make their way to Hamburg, where they would finally start the boat trip to America. It was a wearisome trip by train. And they had only been able to carry one meal. But at each way station—and this train stopped at every town with more than ten houses—a special committee met the immigrants. The steamship company had set up posts to see that travelers did not get waylaid. As soon as the train stopped, the immigrants' committee boarded—with hot tea and cookies. And at each place where the family had to change trains, the immigrants' committee was there to help with the huge bundles that all the Kleegmans carried with them. The trip to Hamburg took three endless days, changing back and forth, even walking across a border to escape over-inquisitive customs guards who weren't very friendly to Jewish immigrants. But finally they came to the ship, a huge ship, the enormous ship, the ship that would take them across two centuries and three thousand miles to the Land of Promises, the Promised Land of Amerika.

And then they were crowded into steerage. Before the boat set sail, the smell and the crowding had already made Elka sick. Israel succumbed soon after. It was midwinter; the trip took three weeks in the heaviest weather. In steerage only a few of the children escaped the chilling sickness that took away all strength and left the passengers lying in their bunks, unable to eat or drink or remember that this was the first leg of a trip into the future.

Hannah was one of the lucky ones.

"It was a wonderful trip, a marvelous trip," she was to remember. "It was the first time in my life I ever had enough to
eat. And what food! Oh, what food!" Of course, the steerage
tables were set up to feed all the passengers. And the few hardy
travelers who made their way to the tables were urged to have
as much as they could eat. To a ghetto child from Borschevka,
to whom boiled potato and pickle were a hearty dinner, this
was more than plenty; this was heaven.

On the first morning she came down to breakfast, there was
only one other person at the table. "Good morning," she said
to the old man already seated. He looked at her. She was cram-
ming a bun smeared with butter into her mouth. "Excuse
me," he said, bowing and leaving the table. She looked a-
round. At each seat there was another of the beautiful buns,
delicious cakelike buns with raisins. "Oh, look," she called,
but there was no one. "Only look, how beautiful!" She gathered all the buns at the table and buttered them carefully. She
was amazed to discover that there was more for breakfast than
buns. A filling porridge, served with milk and more butter
and sugar, real little grains of sugar, like the rich used; because
you could not hold them in your mouth, they had to be
poured into the cup or the bowl. In Borschevka, when
you wanted to say a man was rich you said, "He stirs with a
spoon." Now here was Hannah Kleegman, a bowl of porridge in
front of her, and she was stirring with a spoon.

She finished her porridge and a hot cup of coffee, which she
also stirred with sugar, and left with her hoard of buns.

"Mother, Mother, I have something so beautiful to show
you, you won't believe it."

"I don't think I can raise my head to look at anything, no
matter how beautiful, Hannahle. Let me rest."

"No, look, Mother; look at these. I brought them for you.
You can't be too sick to eat them."

Unwisely, Elka looked. She groaned, turned away, and said

to Hannah: "Don't ever do that again. While we are on the boat, I forbid you to bring me food. If I'm well enough to eat, I'll ask you for food."

"But look, Mother, buns with raisins, many raisins. I counted the raisins in the bun I ate, and there were eighteen! Just look how beautiful."

"Too beautiful to eat, Hannahle. Take them away or eat them yourself."

Israel, too, when she found him, was uninterested in the beautiful buns. And the baby was too small. In the end she ate them all herself. And while she never stopped exclaiming over their beauty, she found that her enthusiasm for the breakfast buns had somehow diminished.

But there was much more than breakfast. There were lunch and supper, too. And at each meal Hannah ate her own food and the food that Elka and Israel and Sophie weren't eating. After all, they were paying for four passages. If she didn't eat it, it was like throwing out money.

No matter what anyone else thought of that rough, turbulent passage, Hannah knew it was heaven, as simple as that. They were warm (with so many people giving off so much body heat in such a small place, they could be nothing else); there was food, such food as she had never seen, so much as she had never imagined existed. And even the officers came down to see that they were all right. Of course, it was too bad Elka was so sick. But she would get better.

In the tightly packed steerage compartments, panic was just under the surface. The sick, bewildered immigrants had never believed they would make it to Amerika. This awful, terrible trip, was it any way to get there? The ship rolled so heavily that they had to tie themselves into their bunks. Already, one or two had taken bad falls. It was not enough that once in a while the officers of the ship would come down and say a few encouraging words. After all, the officers weren't in steerage. They did not know how it was when your belly was aching with hunger, there was food waiting to be eaten, and you were too sick to eat.

Look at them, as they walked through. Big, brawny men who rolled with the ship and didn't even seem to notice. How could they know what this trip was really like? They might joke to the immigrants that no one had ever died of seasickness, people just wished they could. But that was no joke. To be so desperately sick that you wanted to die wasn't funny. Hannah went through the trip happily. But she heard the others; she understood more than most, too.

"We'll never get to dry land," in Russian.

"*Oi,* if only I could die. If only I were dead already," in Yiddish.

"God is punishing me for being so bold. I should never have left my home and my wife," in Polish.

And more, much more, in many languages.

Even Elka said to Hannah: "If I had known what this would be like, I would never have had the courage to leave. Lucky that Meriam and Rachel didn't tell us about it."

The panic grew. Crowded one on top of the other, tempers became uncertain. Fights sprang up among the immigrants. The smallest thing was enough to start them off. A hand would be flung out carelessly—it was a group that expressed themselves as much with their hands as their tongues. A hand would be flung out carelessly and strike someone. In steerage, long before Freud, people understood there were no accidents. A blow was a blow. What had been a joyous hymn to the hope of Amerika had now settled into the sullen mutter of people displaced, dispossessed, afraid that tomorrow would bring only worse.

Then there was a storm. A storm in steerage, where the boat already pitched so badly, where you couldn't stand and you had no room to fall. They lay there tied down to what would surely be their coffins. Too sick, too scared, too resigned even to scream in their terror. Ah! The boat was rolling less. The waves must not be so high. Slowly, slowly they began to hope. Slowly, one and then another head rose above the bunk-sides.

"*Oi!*"

"*Borsha moya!*"

Scream after scream echoed out. There was water all over the floors. The boat had sprung a leak. One or two cool heads rose to take a look.

"It's nothing. On a boat you get wet."

"Don't worry," said someone else, "if the boat were sinking they would stop it to let the rich people off."

They were one week away from New York, and the boat had sprung a leak. After all, the cool heads were right. It wasn't such a bad leak. The first- and second-class passengers never knew about it, even if the boat did slow down a little.

The steerage passengers pretended not to notice that one day the floor had been wet, and the next day they were walking in water, ankle-deep. The ship hadn't sunk yet, not even in that terrible storm. Why should it sink? Prayers began to sound loudly all day long, in many languages, and always to a God who would calm the seas and bring the boat to shore.

The ankle-deep water, though, was rushing through the steerage compartment, creating a small river. And the river began to flow. It flowed through the rush baskets and the straw bags that the peasants had packed their few belongings in, and it flowed through the cargo, too. In the cargo were many bottles of wine, destined for the tables of the rich, but traveling, like the peasants, in steerage.

One by one, corks were dislodged by the flowing flood. And one night a peasant looked down and screamed, screamed hard, loud, on a rising note of fear.

"It is the beginning of the slaughter! They are slaughtering us! We are riding on blood, not water."

And they all looked down at the water they walked in. It was red, the red of spilled blood.

Their screams were heard, even in the first-class dining saloon, where the second sitting was just sitting down.

Down ran the officers who were in charge of steerage morale, the officers who had made jokes about seasickness, who came down once in a while to see that everything was all right, everything was fine. They, too, looked horrified as they waded through the blood-red waters. They dispersed quickly, each to a different compartment to find out what had happened. One stayed in the bunk room, where Hannah was terribly frightened, comforting Elka, telling her it was all right, the ship was moving, nothing could have happened. He heard her voice raised in comfort, it was a small piping voice, but a voice that would always be heard, even over the screams of a crowd.

And then another officer came in.

"It's nothing," he whispered, "some wine kegs have spilled into all this bilge, but we're going to have a panic on our hands. Do something quick."

And the officer did something. "Little girl!" he shouted. "Yes, you. Come here, come with me, and bring your friends."

And Hannah came running, gathering children along the way.

"Look," said the officer, "nothing is wrong; a little wine has spilled into the water. It isn't blood; it's wine, and wine is a reason to rejoice. Listen, sing me a song we can all dance to . . . a dance you know. . . . Let's play marvelous games, right here, right now."

Hannah looked at whom she had there. Yes, there were a few Russian children, and she began a simple children's song, the Russian equivalent of "Ring-Round-the-Rosie." The children were shivering and frightened, they turned quickly to laughter, and its promise of safety. The other officers grabbed their hands, singing in English, laughing and dancing, until they grabbed other hands to bring them into the circle.

Knee-deep in blood-red water, they played singing game after singing game. . . . Sometimes the words were Russian;

sometimes they were Polish; once there was a Norwegian counting-out game . . . and all the children joined in quickly to keep the games going, going, to keep the panic from overwhelming them.

Hand after hand grabbed out and brought another one into the circle; then hands broke, and it became a long, unruly line snaking from crowded cubicle to crowded cubicle, pulling more and more into the group until there were more people dancing and singing than there were lying on the narrow bunks. And as the panic had jumped from person to person, so did the gaiety.

"Come and dance, come and dance," the cry rang out. "We're dancing in wine."

"Come," in shouted Italian, "it's like treading grapes. Dance, dance!"

And the circle went round until they were all exhausted from fear and joy. Slowly it went around and then slower still, as one after another dropped out to fall onto a bunk. At last all that were left, as they had started out, were the children and the officers. And one officer picked Hannah up on his shoulders to whirl her around.

"Well done, well done, little one," he said, "you've done more than you know today. Here's a kiss for you, not from me, but from everyone. They can be grateful to you." And so Hannah brought with her to the new world yet another benediction.

Reb Israel Refuses

THE LEAK WAS FIXED. The wine and the water were pumped away, and soon the land of Amerika was sighted. Excited cries followed one after another: "Amerika! Amerika!" "We're there." "It's there."

Hannah helped Elka and Israel gather together the belongings they had brought. Seasickness and fear alike were forgotten.

The boat steamed past the Statue of Liberty, past Ellis Island, and landed the immigrants at Castle Garden, a place that Hannah—who now speaks unaccented English—still refers to as Kessel Garden. And there the immigrants were set down.

One after another went through Immigration to be sent away to the land of opportunity. The Kleegmans were at the end of an endless line. They watched and waited as the people ahead talked earnestly through interpreters to the customs officials. They saw family after family triumphantly produce the required twenty-five dollars in American money that proved they would not be destitute in their new country. And they heard person after person say, "Why do we have to bring money into a country where gold lies in the streets?"

They felt very superior. What greenhorns to think that gold

lies in the streets! The Kleegmans knew perfectly well that Amerika was like any other country. You had to work to earn money. Meriam and Rachel had worked hard for their twenty-five dollars in earnest money. The only difference was that here you could find the work to earn the money.

No, the Kleegmans were not complete greenhorns. They knew a lot about Amerika. They knew it was bounded on the north by Eighth Street and on the south by Division. They themselves knew where they were going—to Chrystie Street.

They smiled and chatted with the people in front of them. What difference did it make that they spoke Yiddish and the others spoke Swedish? They could understand each other perfectly.

"Look," said Reb Israel, as the people at the head of the line paid their fifty cents for an enormous bread and an enormous salami, Amerika's greeting to immigrants who had to march on their stomachs until they found their footing. "In Amerika we'll never be hungry." *"Ja, ja,"* with a smile, was the answer. An answer anyone could understand.

Finally, the Kleegmans were almost at the head of the line. They straightened up. They gathered their bundles. No one was here to meet them because no one had been sure when they would get here or exactly what boat they would take. The detour through Austria had taken time. Bad weather had delayed them further. But it didn't matter. Reb Israel knew exactly where they were going. He clutched Meriam's last letter in his hand with the address printed in English for the customs men.

Then their moment came. They were at the big table, where huge registers were open to record the arrival of a good part of Europe to America's hospitable shores.

The interpreter came over to them. Laboriously he took from Reb Israel the necessary details. It was very hard. The interpreter spoke a heavily accented Yiddish, and his accent was from another country. Reb Israel had had less trouble

understanding his Swedish co-travelers. Such simple questions as "What's your name?" required an elaborate pantomime. At the same time, the interpreter indicated with great
skill that he would be in trouble if Reb Israel showed that he
couldn't understand the Yiddish. Who was Reb Israel to get
the interpreter into trouble?

"What's he talking, Father?" asked Hannah, who was too
short to see the winks and gestures that accompanied each
question. "It's because of your slanty eyes. They think you're
Chinese. Ask for a Jewish interpreter."

"*Sha, sha,* Hannahle. They think he's talking Jewish. You'll
make him lose his job!"

And Reb Israel went back to the difficult task of making
himself understood to a man who seemed, indeed, to be talking Chinese Yiddish.

But after a while it wasn't so funny. Something was wrong.
The Swedes had gone through after answering a few simple
questions, with answers that were recorded in the book. Their
papers had been stamped. They were through. But the immigration official was not writing down Reb Israel's answers in
the book. He just looked up and kept asking questions. The
questions were all about Sophie. He kept pointing to her and
asking the same thing again and again, then shaking his head.
Reb Israel started using pantomime. He couldn't understand
what the interpreter was asking, but he did his best. What
about Sophie? The interpreter rocked an imaginary baby in
his arms, and then shook his head. Reb Israel nodded. After
all, Sophie certainly was a baby. They certainly had rocked
her. Then the interpreter pointed to Elka, and shook his head
even harder. He made a face and shrugged his shoulders. Finally, the interpreter pointed to Reb Israel, rocked the baby,
and shook his head.

Reb Israel could make nothing of any of it. What was wrong
with Sophie that they were all coming to look at her and shake
their heads? She was a beautiful baby with Elka's own curling

ringlets of blond hair. Obligingly she opened her eyes and smiled at the interpreter, who kept on shaking his head.

The line behind them got restless. Already they had taken enough time for three ordinary families to go through. Not unkindly, the interpreter pulled them away, letting the people behind go through. Earnestly he talked to Reb Israel. A long speech with much pointing to the baby and to Elka and a lot more shaking of his head.

Reb Israel turned to Hannah: "See if you can understand anything he says, Hannahle. Maybe he speaks one of the other languages you speak." But Hannah knew that was hopeless. After all, if he spoke Russian or German, they'd be able to understand his Yiddish.

Still, she tried each of her languages in turn. All she got was a blank stare and more pointing and noddings.

Finally, an exasperated customs official came up to them and grabbed Sophie, as if he were planning to take her away. That they all understood, and there was a huge babble of outraged Yiddish, supported by the people behind them, who also didn't know what was going on but were more than ready to take Reb Israel's part.

Where did they think they were taking Sophie? Wherever it was, interpreter, father, mother, sister, with all the bundles, followed, running as fast as they could, as encumbered as they were.

They went into a little room set apart. The customs official who had grabbed Sophie talked for a long time to the interpreter. The interpreter turned and made many gestures to Reb Israel, talking all the time. Reb Israel turned to Elka.

How could they give an answer when they didn't know the question?

The customs official threw his hands up in disgust. He shook his head. He turned to Reb Israel and beckoned him along.

They all trailed out of the room with their bundles, but this time Elka had both arms around Sophie. At least they had gotten the baby back from the immigration man.

Then they were taken into another large room. The interpreter left them. He indicated that he had done all he could for them, and was sorry it hadn't turned out better. And he made a universal symbol, one they all understood. He drew his forefinger across his throat.

What was happening? Were they being sent back to Russia for a reason they didn't even know about? What was this big room where they were standing? Above all, why had the interpreter given the signal of a cut throat?

"With an interpreter like that, you don't need a tongue," joked Reb Israel, trying to lift up Hannah and Elka's spirits. Sophie, oblivious to the troubles she was causing, had found another tiny child to play with.

Just then a man came up to them carrying a piece of chalk. He seized Reb Israel by the shoulder and spoke loudly to him, but in what language? When Reb Israel didn't answer, the man turned him around firmly and drew on his back with the chalk. Then he took Elka by the arm, turned her around, and drew on her back with the chalk. Reb Israel watched as the man made a big X. When he pulled Hannah up and marked her with an X, Reb Israel began to yell.

"What are you doing? Stop it! Stop it this minute!" Never had Hannah seen him so upset.

The man paid no attention, marked the baby, and went on his way. They saw he was marking everyone in the room the same way.

"Elka," said Reb Israel, "pick up the baby. Take your bundles. Hannahle, take what you can. Come on. It's not too late. We are going back on that boat, right now."

"But why, Father? Why do you want to go back?"

"It is too late for Rachel and Meriam. They allowed this terrible thing to happen to them. After all, they are only young girls. But to us it will not happen. Nothing in Russia is worse than this."

"But, Father, what's so bad? Do you know what's happening?"

Reb Israel was gathering everything up. He handed Hannah a bundle. "Of course I know what's happening. What's on your back and your mother's back and my back and even the baby's back? God forgive us, it's a cross. You know why they won't let us in? They are trying to convert us. Not even for Amerika will we become Christians."

Hannah was in total despair. Nothing would convince Reb Israel to convert. But how could this be so? All the people in this room had an X on their backs. Yet surely they weren't all Jewish. Some of them looked like complete foreigners. And the little boy Sophie had found to play with was walking around without clothes, and it was quite obvious that his religion had never required a ritual circumcision.

"Nonsense, nonsense." Elka's voice sounded in the babble strong and sure. "Would our daughters ever have us come to a country which would make us convert? Even if they were willing to become *goyim,* which God forbid they never would, they know you. They grew up with you. No one would ever imagine that such a pious Jew would become a Christian. It's nonsense, Israel. You've misunderstood."

"While this cross stays on our backs, we will not go on to Amerika. I go no further, not one step."

"So stay. You have money? Give me some." Elka went around the room, looking and looking for someone to talk to, to find out why they were in this big room instead of in Amerika.

She came back. "I don't understand. But, Israel, it is not conversion. There are plenty of good Christians here. One woman says she's here because she caught a bad cold on the boat and now she can't stop coughing. Another said she lost her papers. It is something holding us up, something we don't understand. But we have to stay here now until someone vouches for us. We have to get hold of Meriam or Rachel. How can we do it? One woman over there said that her daughter told her when she came, she should put a notice in the Jewish paper. You pay some money, they print whatever you say. In Yiddish, so anyone can read it."

"So how do we get to the Jewish paper? Here we are in a room, we don't even know where; we don't even know if it's in Amerika. Where will you find the Jewish paper?"

"There's a man over there. He took my money. He's putting it in the Jewish paper. It will say that any relatives of Israel and Elka Kleegman from Borschevka should come to help them at Castle Garden. See, there he goes out. And I found out what the crosses are. It has nothing to do with Christians. It just means with that cross on your back you can't go out of this room."

So Reb Israel and Elka and Hannah and Sophie sat down to wait for the notice in the Jewish paper to reach Rachel and Meriam. They waited; they slept. Someone came through with slices of bread and cheese. They waited; they slept. Someone came through with coffee. They waited; they slept. Someone came through calling Israel Kleegman, Elka Kleegman, Israel Kleegman, Elka Kleegman. It was Hannah who heard the call. She woke up Israel. "Father, Father, they are calling you. Wake up. Wake up. They're calling you!" Hannah woke them all, got them together, and chased the man to the other side of the room.

"We're here. Right here." Of course he didn't understand them, but he repeated. "Kleegman? Kleegman?" Reb Israel nodded. They followed him into another official office.

There stood a man none of them recognized. But the minute he opened his mouth, they all fell on him. He spoke Yiddish. Borschevka Yiddish!

Once again they were subject to winks and nods and frowns

that the immigration men could not see. But these winks were quickly intelligible.

"Hello, Cousin Israel," said the stranger. "I am sorry I was not down to meet you. I have told the immigration authorities that you are my cousin and that I can vouch for you. Now they want to ask you a few questions."

Reb Israel immediately let loose a storm of questions of his own. What was the trouble? Why were there crosses on his family's backs? Did the Americans want to convert him? What did they mean by trying to take the baby away?

"You'll know all the answers soon. Now, just do as I tell you. There's nothing to worry about; it's just a little misunderstanding. Sh-sh-sh." The stranger continued. "They want to know if Sophie is really your child. Your wife is too old to have such a young child. They think you must be smuggling her in."

"No, no, she's our child; tell them she's our child. Look, right here are the papers. See, she was born when my wife was fifty."

The stranger turned around to the immigration officials and talked to them for a long time.

"Forgive me," he said, "but they don't believe your wife is only in her fifties. To them she looks much older." Oh, Elka of the golden curls, turned by life into an old, old woman, but a woman who, to her death at eighty-five would still have the spirit to dance at every family gathering, who spoke to us in sparkling rhymes, and made up marvelous songs for her grandchildren . . . and got down on her knees to scrub the floors after the maids had finished an inept job.

"But here are her papers, too, you see. Look, it says here how old she is. Sophie is our youngest child. Explain it to them."

There was much talking back and forth, but finally the immigration men began writing down in their books.

"Name?"

"Israel Kleegman. This is my family. Elka Kleegman, Hannah Kleegman, Sophie Kleegman."

"Do you have enough money to feed your family until you
find work?"

"Here is the twenty-five dollars."

"Sign here."

And then, finally, it was done. Almost done. Israel would
not leave.

"Come on, come on," said the stranger.

"No," said Israel.

"What's the matter?"

"Why are there crosses on our backs?"

"But those aren't crosses! Those are exes. They just mean
that you are not allowed through. If there's any trouble, they
mark you with an ex on the back so everyone can see you're
not allowed through. Come on, come on."

And off they went to Chrystie Street with the stranger, who
wasn't a stranger at all but the brother-in-law of Moishe Weiss,
from Borschevka, who had heard many great tales of Reb
Israel Kleegman and had come down as soon as he read that a
landtsman was in trouble.

How Golden Was Amerika!

WHAT A LIFE they were coming to! Some ways more golden than even they had imagined! Meriam and Rachel had found a small apartment on Chrystie Street, after much looking at six in the morning. That was the only time. Work started at six thirty or seven and lasted far into the night. And night was too dark. What could you tell about an apartment in the dark? So the two sisters had hunted and hunted to find a light apartment. It was four and a half very small rooms, but there was an indoor bathroom on the landing below. An indoor bathroom to share with only three other families. What luxury for Borschevkans!

Elka looked around and frowned. There was just enough room. No room for hospitality. And none at all for the boarders she planned to take in.

The girls were bursting with news. With the great things that were Amerika. With the new life, the good life, the life of peace. *Lachiam toiveem sholem:* that had been Borschevka's favorite toast. And here it was.

True, Meriam and Rachel worked incredibly hard from early morning till eight at night and then brought home piecework. But after work, what times there were to be had! Great times for the whole family. On the Lower East Side there was a bustling, burgeoning new cultural life for the immigrants. Hardly a night went by that there wasn't within a few blocks' walk, a lecture, a concert, a play to see. Most of them were free. And with only Meriam's and Rachel's meager earnings, the rent to pay and the family to feed, zero was the amount in the entertainment budget. But what did that matter? Debates were free. Profound intellectual discussions, lectures on the benefits of Socialism, the evils of Socialism, the educational theories of Rousseau and Dewey, the reasons why New York must elect this or that politician to office. Discussion groups, literary groups, clubs formed by immigrants who had come from villages around Borschevka, free opera and free musicales. The Lower East Side offered its newcomers a dizzying round of pleasures and a schism. All they had to do was take sides.

They had a choice. They could be orthodox and immure themselves in the Torah and the Talmud just as they had in Europe. Or they could catch fire from the spirit of freedom and free enterprise. Some combined both and became orthodox capitalists, while others took on revolutionary fervor and became Socialists, fighters, reformers. For the Kleegmans there was no conflict. Israel stayed with his heart, and turned more and more to the Talmud. The others found Amerika had everything. New fields of intellectual exploration, new ways to be free. They went to every lecture, read every book, and all of them, even Elka, shed the shibboleths of orthodox Judaism as soon as they were able. But none of them wanted to hurt or defy Israel. At home they lived as they had in Borschevka, though abroad they were Americans.

Especially Meriam, oh, Meriam was a beauty. And a firebrand! Her perfect oval face was framed by dark, dark hair. She was a constant reminder that the first Madonna was, after all, Jewish, and her plump figure suited the voluptuous styles of the times. As soon as she started to work in the terrible sweatshops of the shirt factory where girls worked fourteen

hours a day six days a week, she discovered that there were
people fighting. She did not dare join the rebels until the family was safely here in Amerika. But the day the Kleegmans
landed, she felt it was safe to join the organizers of the shirt
factories.

Poor, shy, deafened Rachel was a pretty girl, too. By today's
standards—with her doe eyes and uptilted nose—the pretti-
est of the lot. She attracted many boys. She was always ready to
say something pleasant, just to show her intentions were good
even if her hearing wasn't.

For Reb Israel, the golden land remained somehow a land
beyond his reach. While the others found good fights to fight,
equality, better living conditions, higher education for
women—he found himself only in alien corn. He was invited
to be the rabbi, the *reb,* and the resident wise man of a local
shul. It was a position of great honor, offered to him because
his reputation had preceded him from Borschevka. He went
to one meeting at the synagogue, saw the young men with
their clean-shaven cheeks and short hair, some of them even
hatless in the House of God, and turned down the job with a
gentle question:

"Among such *goyim,*" he said, "what need is there for a
rabbi?"

Instead he took a job as a presser at a huge one-hundred-
pound press. He stood all day, bending under its weight. "It's
good," he said; "it leaves my mind free for the important
things." And his free mind wandered contentedly over Talmudic arguments and proofs.

Elka, for the moment, could employ nothing but her mind.
Her apartment was too small to take in boarders, though she
was constantly feeding newcomers who had just arrived. She
didn't have the capital for a store. But, like her daughters, she
took to the new ideas of Amerika like *pais* to a *Yeshivabucher.*

Israel knew his Elka. He sympathized with her reaction to
the freedom of Amerika, though he couldn't share it or even

admit it to himself. But how he understood Elka! He began to
have unquiet feelings when he left the house early on Saturday
morning to go to what he now called the *"shul* of the *goyim."*
Serving a hot meal on Saturday was absolutely forbidden, for
Saturday was a day of complete rest, the Shabbus that had been
inviolable in Borschevka. Yet he had an uneasy feeling that,
should he return home unexpectedly, he would find the entire
family eating one of the good American meals that were still
such a novelty. When Elka discovered that Israel was feeling
the stove to see if it was hot, the second he came back from *shul*
in the afternoon, she simply made the main meal (of course a
hot one) at breakfast time. The girls had a Shabbus breakfast
that left them unable to move the rest of the day. It was Elka's
new way of keeping the Sabbath.

No one worked on the Shabbus, even if they did eat hot
meals. No one but Rachel. Rachel's job at a men's-wear factory
paid her by the piece. She got so she could never sit down
without a pile of vests at her feet. (Vests were the easiest piecework to take home, they were so portable.) Surely that factory
must have produced a rare innovation in men's suits—with
all the extras Rachel did at home—the two-vest suit. Only
when Israel was looking directly at her on Shabbus could
Rachel make her hands stay still.

With a family of pretty young girls there were bound to be
young men. Mostly they hung around Meriam of the Madonna face and the crusading instincts. But her criteria for
suitors were pretty high. A boy had to approve of her union
sympathies; he had to be a fighter, too. And he had to be in a
good enough position to contribute substantially to the support
of her family.

There was Hannah to put through school. Not like everyone else, not just through grade school, but through high
school, college, and medical school. Sophie, too, would have to
have an education, though it was hard to look at the golden-
haired baby of the family and imagine her education as a seri-

ous financial drain. And any suitor had to "fit": to be able to discuss Talmud with Reb Israel and union organizing with Meriam's friends.

Amongst the beaus who did qualify was a real *landtsman,* the son of a Borschevkan. He was a learned rabbinical student, a *Yeshivabucher,* who had come to Amerika long before the Kleegmans and was making a pretty good living as a butcher —eighteen dollars a week. But he couldn't forget the hard times. He was such a frugal man with a dollar that his winter coat was a bargain bought off a pushcart. What did he care that he was small and the coat was big? However, wherever he went, the difference in size between himself and his coat was noticed. The family began to call him the *Coit mit Longe Armen,* the Coat with the Long Arms. His courtship was assiduous. And ardent. Until one day the Coat with Long Arms took a good look around at the people in Meriam's family: the young ones who had to be educated, the old ones who would have to be supported. He went off quietly and married a pretty blonde who was an only child and had a dowry to bestow on a Talmudic student with a good job.

Still, Meriam and Rachel laughed and enjoyed. One suitor more or less, one burden more or less. This was Amerika. The land was golden and so was the future.

And what about Hannahle, the little wonder? At first she seemed neither so little nor so wonderful. Amerika was a shock. Hannahle was twelve, tiny for her age but much too big for first grade in an American public school. What was she doing there? Her Russian schooling, even in a peasant's public school, had been excellent. But in 1906 the Board of Education had never heard of a foreign-speaking education program. You came to Amerika, you went to school in English, and, if you didn't understand, you stayed in first grade until you did.

For the first time in her life, tiny Hannah was a lummox, among the six- and seven-year-old first-graders. Was this

Amerika? What good was a free school where you couldn't even learn? Hannah thought and thought. Thinking didn't help. You had to do. If she knew five words of English today, she would learn twenty tomorrow. And she would refuse to speak anything else, at home or in the store where she had to work after school to help the family pay back the crushing debt of the passage money.

First came the English. Then came marvelous things, things she'd never learned in Russia: calculus, chemistry, physics. Hannah, hungry for knowledge, literally devoured her lessons, and went from first to eighth grade in five months, and all through high school in two years. Class valedictorian, she struggled desperately over her speech to get rid of a persistent accent that took the worst from all the languages she spoke.

"How can I lead the oath of allegiance?" she said desperately to Meriam, who was a sympathetic but uncomprehending audience. (Nobody minded if Meriam's stirring speeches at union meetings were delivered in an accent.) "When I say it, it comes out 'one nation indiwisible, vith liberty and justice for all'!" wailed Hannah.

Hannah completed all the courses the high school had to offer at the end of two years, and while her principal was worrying about how to fill up her next two she solved the problem very neatly. She won a New York State Regents Scholarship Examination that carried with it automatic acceptance to any state-supported college or university. A hasty adjustment changed her age from fifteen to sixteen in order to complete the college's entrance requirements, and she was admitted to Cornell.

Here was her happy ending: admission to a famous college with a great medical school. But then reality caught up with Hannahle. She had made everything happen just the way she had dreamed. Could she live the dream? No. The scholarship paid her tuition. She had a job waiting on tables to pay room and board. But there was no money left over to contribute to the family. Could she ask Meriam to go on turning down offers of marriage? Or Rachel to slave her life away piece by piece? Maybe the family would have to depend on little Sophie to carry out the dream of Amerika. Hannah went out quietly and began looking for a job. She went to her high-school principal, Miss Carpenter, for help. And Ida May Carpenter, unable to touch a wand to the pumpkin for her Jewish Cinderella, came up with a fairy godfather instead.

He was a philanthropist named Upjohn who was especially interested in young doctors, since he himself had wanted to become a doctor but could only afford to go to pharmacy school. He founded a famous pharmaceutical firm and became a great doer of good.

For Hannah he did the best. He offered to pay all her extra expenses at college and give her a generous allowance besides. In the end, she didn't accept quite as much help as Mr. Upjohn was willing to give. She borrowed $1,000, spread over five years. She sent that all home to the family. And she went off to Cornell convinced that indeed Amerika was a country where anyone could do anything if they wished hard enough, worked hard enough, and knew inside themselves it would happen. How golden was her Amerika—where if money didn't grow on trees, millionaire philanthropists did!

That is the end of Hannah the Borschevkan. Hannah and Hannahle somehow got lost at Cornell. The girl who was found was tiny, with slanting eyes that made her look Japanese, although their sparkle was anything but inscrutable. She had long auburn hair that shed pins wherever she went, and fell down whenever she got excited, which was nearly all the time. Her pale, beautiful skin flushed quickly with pleasure or enthusiasm. Her name was Anna, not Hannah—-Anna Kleegman, the girl who would turn into my mother, the doctor.

Anna, Mary, and Rae— and America

IT WAS A NEW WORLD, and all the girls needed new names. Hannahle became Anna, Meriam—Mary, Rachel—Rae. And life became American.

Where the memories of Borschevka are nearly always memories of tragedy, the Kleegmans' America took on a high comic tone. There were the spirited goings-on of four pretty and lively girls. There was the excitement of change. In Borschevka things were bad; in America, no matter how bad things got, they were good.

In the middle of Anna's last year of high school, while preparations were being made to get her off to Cornell, the family had made the move from Chrystie Street to a huge seven-room apartment at Seventh Street and Avenue B. It was a railroad flat, and immediately posed a dilemma. Since it contained their first private bathroom at the very end of the seven rooms, which rooms should the boarders have?

If they got the rooms closest to the bathroom, everyone else would have to walk through to use those most necessary utilities. If they had the rooms closest to the entrance, how would they get to the bathroom? It was a dilemma that even the Talmudic reasoning of Israel couldn't solve. In fact, until the Kleegmans moved all the way uptown, many years later, boarders were still being shifted, as Elka always said, "to make you much more comfortable."

The Seventh Street apartment was advertised as a cold-water flat, which Elka was assured meant that there was hot water but no heat. For a while, through some fluke, it offered plenty of both, sending up steam during the hottest August New York had ever officially recorded. Then, starting in November, it offered no heat or hot water for the rest of the time they lived there.

Still, it was big enough to house the four girls, Elka and Israel, four boarders, and whatever newcomers were trying to get settled. And whatever hungry people Elka came across in the street.

Money wasn't only tight. It had to be squeezed like a lemon. When Elka's charities did not exceed her board money from the tenants, she could contribute to the family income. But this wasn't often. Israel's salary as a presser would never get any bigger. Rae was the steady earner with her piecework. Mary made the biggest salary, but she was a Kleegman and therefore a dreamer. Her dream was for better wages and working conditions for everyone. Not for nothing did she go to all those lectures. A firebrand, a troublemaker. An *organizer*. Even though she worked under three different names, her employers found her out. And in the big strike of 1910, when Mary actually organized the workers and got her shirt-waist factory into the Cloakmakers' Union, Mary's second-in-command was the boss's son! No one wanted to hire her.

But every offer Anna and Sophie made to give up their education and go to work was met with the most fervent opposition. Go ahead and work, they were told. Work at school. That's your business. In the end, you'll support us all. And in the end they did.

Anna Cooks Dinner

ANNA'S FIRST YEAR at Cornell was a rare one of academic humility. She had to work very hard. The lacunae in her education began to show. For the first time, everyone she was in school with seemed pretty remarkable, and she no longer was a *kleine wunder*. She lacked a basic frame of reference natural to the rest of the students. As Anna said, "It's all Greek to me, only worse. Greek I understand."

By her second year, she had made a number of good friends, a lot of good marks, and was enjoying a considerable success with pre-med men. With her Gibson-girl hairdo and her middie blouse and skirt, she looked like a very young child. Only her mind was all grown up.

One of her new friends invited her to a Thanksgiving vacation away from school and books, complete with a real American Thanksgiving dinner. Anna so looked forward to the treat that when her friend Sarah Jamison was inconsiderate enough to come down with measles two days before the holiday, she sent Anna off to the Jamison farm anyway.

The Jamisons welcomed her warmly. Mrs. Jamison quickly moved her into a kitchen that smelled marvelously of baking, sizzling, roasting and frying, simmering and boiling. Anna smiled. The smell of good cooking was international. This was the way Elka's New York apartment smelled for days before a *Seder,* the traditional Jewish spring feast.

Mrs. Jamison knew enough about feeling strange in a place to put Anna right to work stringing beans for supper. She poured forth a stream of woman talk, particularly about how she was going to cook the turkey tomorrow by a secret recipe that had been handed down from her grandmother to her mother, from her mother to her, which she would in good time impart to Sarah.

The easy chatter put Anna completely at ease. But her mauling of the string beans showed that however bright she might be in a classroom, she was no genius in the kitchen.

Mrs. Jamison gently took away the string beans and started Anna chopping onions for the sage and giblet dressing that was going into the turkey that very evening.

"Part of the secret," said Mrs. Jamison, "is to put the stuffing in well ahead of time so it has a chance to season the bird."

The two continued with preparations for that day's dinner and the next day's feast, but Anna noticed she was never allowed to stay long at any culinary chore. As a cook, it was clear, Anna was going to be an absolutely sensational doctor. But everything was so nearly ready and so well planned that there was almost nothing to do. Anna could set the table, which was all the help Mrs. Jamison really needed.

The farmhands started coming in for dinner. They sat down, still rosy and damp from a good pump cleaning, to a marvelous meal, one that made Anna wonder what could possibly be in store for them tomorrow. For once Anna was reduced to total silence. There was a huge group of hands, there for a late apple harvest, and she and Mrs. Jamison were the only women. Although the men could not be said to be talkative, the sheer weight of numbers made their deep voices, asking for the rolls or the butter or more gravy, oppressive. There were four Jamison sons, Mr. Jamison, eleven farmhands, and seven boarders, who helped out with chores, too.

Then disaster struck. Mrs. Jamison fell, bringing in the deep-dish apple pie. One leg was folded under the poor woman in a position no leg had a right to hold. Anna looked frantically for Mr. Jamison in that sea of anguished men. "Go get the doctor, quickly! She's broken that leg."

When Mrs. Jamison's leg had been set and splinted, the lady herself was given a powerful sedative, and put to bed in an up-stairs bedroom. Anna, who had acted as nurse and comforter while all this was going on, saw Mrs. Jamison looking at her dubiously. Anna assured her: "Don't worry about a thing. I'll get everything ready for Thanksgiving. You'll see. It will be delicious."

Anna made her tones ringing, her demeanor so assured that Mrs. Jamison would not remember the mangled string beans, the chopped onions that had been squashed beyond recogni-tion, the other cooking chores Anna could not manage.

"Well," Mrs. Jamison said, "I suppose I can tell you how to cook the turkey, and you can do the rest."

"Of course," said Anna soothingly.

"Have you ever cooked a turkey?" Mrs. Jamison asked.

"Certainly," Anna said bravely.

"Well, in that case it will be easy enough. Everything is done already except for the turkey and the vegetables. The pies, the slaw, the relishes—I've been making those all week."

And she started telling Anna what was to be served when and just what course went with what. Finally she fell asleep.

At five the next morning Anna was already in the kitchen, racking her brain. She had seen Elka boil chickens, and that gave delicious chicken soup, especially with homemade noodles . . . but obviously she couldn't boil that huge turkey. The fact was, she'd never cooked anything in her life. It was Elka's belief that she had come to America in order to save her girls from the drudgery of housework. So, while Mary and Rachel had picked up the rudiments of cooking and keeping a house clean on the theory that they might have to take care of a husband someday, the two youngest girls didn't know how to boil water.

Mrs. Jamison, wide awake and worried, called down: "One of my tricks is to put the turkey in a very low oven and let it cook all day long. Put the vegetables in after about eight hours and let them roast for another two, keep on basting it every quarter hour and sprinkle it with a little seasoning every time you baste. You'll find my special seasoning in the box on the stove. The box that has a hen on it."

"All right. I'll do just what you told me. Don't worry a bit about it."

Anna looked helplessly around. You cooked a turkey in the oven, but in what? Certainly there was no pot big enough to hold the bird. Just then another call came from the bedroom:

"You'll find the roasting pan under the sink, on the shelf all the way to the right."

Anna looked on the shelf all the way to the right. All she could see was a big dishpan with a cover. And it was black. All her mother's cooking pots were bright and shiny. So were all the pots in this spotless kitchen. She looked all around, then shrugged her shoulders helplessly and pulled out the black dishpan. Well, the turkey certainly fitted into it very nicely.

"Make sure the stitches where I sewed up the bird are holding," the voice from upstairs called. Well, a pre-med should practice surgical stitches. She took the needle and thread that had been carefully placed on the shelf over the sink, and proceeded to do an experimental suturing job. Emboldened by this obviously successful effort—those stitches would hold through Hades, if need be—she looked around for the vegetables that were to accompany the bird. Let's see, there were beautiful new potatoes—no point in peeling them, their skins were the merest translucency over them . . . and carrots, scrubbed—well, they should be sliced somehow . . . and there were beautiful whole onions—Anna loved onions— and red radishes already cut into roses. The turnips were mashed, so they couldn't go in—they needed heating or something before serving—but how about a few of those juicy red apples? After all, they couldn't hurt.

Slowly but surely she piled up an incongruous group of vegetables in the pan. Then she lighted the oven, set the flame low, and started the turkey cooking. The smell that soon wafted through the house was so delicious that she hoped for the best—an attitude with which she always faced life anyway.

After a while, she started setting the festive table—putting out all the pies, relishes, and savories that had been prepared for weeks. She thought regretfully of the eight beautiful loaves of homemade bread that had been planned for the meal and had risen dutifully—but after all, one had to recognize one's limitations; homemade bread was certainly the limit!

When she opened up the oven she realized she couldn't tell a thing from looking, so she poured a little of the pan gravy over the turkey, as she'd seen her mother do with a roast, and shut the door. As Elka was fond of saying, "When you have plenty of food there's no trick to cooking." Well, there was certainly plenty of food here—it should all be good.

The men went off to a special late church service, but they would be back soon. Anna looked at the turkey again. It didn't look too much like the cooked chickens she'd seen, so she made the oven a little hotter. Still, it smelled marvelous!

Time was hanging heavy on her hands. She loaded a plate with all the already prepared goodies and took that up to Mrs. Jamison, who seemed still to be under the influence of the sedative the doctor had given her. Mrs. Jamison stirred, opened her eyes, said, "Thank you," weakly, and then sat bolt upright.

"What's that smell, Anna?"

"That's my turkey, cooking slowly just like you told me to cook it."

"Well, it doesn't smell like any turkey I ever cooked. What did you put in it?"

"Mrs. Jamison, you cook your turkey according to an ancient family recipe. Well, I'm cooking mine the way we used to do it in Borschevka. My mother wouldn't let me tell you what I put in it."

"H-m-m-m. Well, it's unusual—I'll say that. Did you put in cabbage?"

"No," said Anna, trying to remember, "no, no cabbage."

"Still, it smells *good*. And after all, the boys can have my turkey any time. This will be a pleasant change for them."

"Yes, I'm sure it will be a change," said Anna.

She rushed down the stairs to take another look. Ah, the bird was browning nicely. Cooking was a joke, as easy as anything. She made the oven a little hotter, poured a little more of the juices from the pan over the whole thing, wondered what did smell like cabbage, and forgot about it. What could be bad?

Finally, the men came back. Mr. Jamison came over to Anna. "How's our chief cook and bottle washer? All ready to give us a great feed? Good! We're all going to wash up and sit right down. Then we'll see what you can dish up for us."

They all sat down to the table, heads bowed in grace, eyes searching for the nearest steaming platter.

Anna went back in and took out the turkey. It was awfully brown now. In fact, it was black. She looked at the huge turkey platter she had prepared, and then realized she had no idea how to get the turkey onto it. She shrugged. Why not take it to the table in the dishpan? Let Mr. Jamison worry about getting it out.

She took a deep breath, picked up the dishpan, and brought it in to the table. Mr. Jamison looked at it a little dubiously. "Kind of brown, isn't it?"

"Well, that's a special way I cook it," said Anna, "crisp on the outside."

"Smells . . . interesting," he said.

The other men had already begun to eat all the side dishes

and trimmings. They looked eagerly at the main course, sitting there waiting to be carved. Mr. Jamison, Anna noticed, got the bird out of the pan and onto the platter with no difficulty. He started carving expertly. Then he got to her sutures. "Say," he said, "I don't know who closed this bird up, but she sure didn't intend for me to get it open!" After a prolonged struggle the sutures gave way, and a magnificent aroma—Mrs. Jamison's special family stuffing, spilled out.

"Where's the gravy?" asked Mr. Jamison.

"In the pan," said Anna. Were you supposed to *make* gravy?

The first pieces of turkey were being given out, along with the gravy from the pan and a kind of boiled-away rubble that Anna realized were all her beautiful vegetables cooked down and out.

Anna held her breath. She waited for the first bites to go down. At least no one was spitting it out or choking. No one said anything, either. They just ate and ate and ate.

As far as Anna could see, everyone was eating everything just the way they always ate. In silence and with dedication. She quietly passed her plate and got some turkey and gravy back. Well, *she* thought it was good, no matter what anybody said. Or didn't say. Unusual. But good.

She noticed that all the turkey *went*. Still there was no comment as she cleared, and passed pieces of pie. Indeed, the only praise she heard at that table was the praise to the Lord in the Thanksgiving grace. As she got up to start clearing, Mr. Jamison said, "Thanks Anna. You did very well; we appreciate that." There was a vague rumble from down the table that might have been agreement.

"Well," said Mr. Jamison, as they all got up, "you've had a lot of work to do today, Anna. I'll send some of the boys in to help you clear up." Obviously, he felt this was a great concession. Anna would have been just as happy to let the boys clear it all up. But she knew what was expected of her.

She was up to her elbows in soapsuds when the first of the

boys came in. He put down the dishes, and without so much as a "Hello" said, "Miss Kleegman, I wonder if you'd marry me."

Anna was so startled she dropped a dish.

"I couldn't have heard you," she said. "What did you say?"

"Well, Miss Kleegman, I've never in my life tasted a meal like that. I just wonder if you'd marry me. You are a wonderful woman. Yes, ma'am, and I would be very proud if you'd marry me."

Anna decided that the boys must have had something more than a church service before lunch. She smiled pleasantly and said: "Well, you know, Mr.—Uh—I have two more years of college and three years of medical school before I get married. And then I have to do my training in the hospital. By that time I'm sure you'll have a pretty wife and a lot of darling children, and a farm of your own."

Mr. Uh was so overwhelmed at the mention of his future progeny that he left precipitously, making way for another farmhand bearing dishes.

"Miss Kleegman, are you engaged?" asked this one.

"No, I'm not." Anna replied. She was beginning to get nervous.

"Well, if you can treat a man the way you did that turkey, I would like to be that man. I've never tasted anything so good in all my days." Anna explained that she had no designs on either men or turkeys. By this time she was somewhat surprised when the next farmhand left off his dishes without proposing.

She received fourteen proposals that day: all four sons of the house, eight farmhands, and two boarders. And every one of them mentioned the turkey as a basis for an idyllic relationship. She always regretted that she hadn't written her recipe down. Later in her life, when she became an ardent matchmaker, she felt that that day's secret formula could have taken every one of her hopeless old maids off her hands.

This Little Piggie Wasn't Kosher

THE JAMISONS were so appreciative of the feast that Anna had made for their Thanksgiving that they invited her back many times. Indeed, she began to seem like a second daughter to them, and it was with great regret that they realized that she had really meant it when she turned down, one after another, all their sons. Nothing would have pleased them more than to welcome her into the family. Mr. Jamison, on one of her frequent visits, took her aside to tell her how she had really been made to be a farm wife.

"If you want to go into medicine, why not become a veterinarian?" he persisted. "Cornell has one of the best veterinary schools in the country. I'll grant you, it's a little unusual for a woman, but then you'll be dealing with something reliable— you can always count on how *animals* will behave."

While he didn't actually *say* there was something basically inferior about treating human beings, there was no doubt in Anna's mind what he meant.

She became quite adept at chores, and the Jamisons racked their brains for some way to pay her back for her many helpful trips to the farm.

That's why, on Seventh Street, three days before *Pesach,* the Jewish Easter, a huge crate was delivered to Anna Kleegman, all the way from the upstate farm. The crate filled the tiny room.

"Be careful you don't keep it out too long," said the grinning farmhand who delivered it. "It's special for Easter. It belongs in the icebox."

Elka, who was home with Sophie, looked at the huge crate and at her icebox. It would have been easier to put the box in the crate.

Oh, well, Anna would be home soon. She carefully went about her Passover preparations. While Israel had accustomed himself to many of the changes he had to make in America, he was still strictly kosher, and would allow no laxness, no oversight, in the *Pesach* ritual. Everything had to be specially cleaned and freshened. It was a nuisance to have to have four sets of dishes and pots and silver for everything. Elka, becoming more and more of an iconoclast, would not have bothered, but this was Israel's way of keeping in touch with his past. And to him it was all-important. After all, nothing that gave Elka an excuse to clean up everything could be anything but good.

Mary came home and immediately fell over the huge box. "What's that Mother?"

"*Vus veiss ich?* What do I know? Something for Anna from the farm. She'd better come home soon, or the man said it would spoil. In the icebox I certainly don't have room."

Rae came in next. She, too, fell over the crate, which was awkwardly placed near the door. She, too, heard all the explanations.

Finally, Anna came home. As she tumbled into the door over the huge crate, everyone said in chorus, "Don't ask us, Anna; it's for you, from the farm."

"Isn't that sweet of the Jamisons?" said Anna. "It must be something special for Passover." She got a carving knife from the kitchen and began attacking the wires that held the crate together. Slowly and painfully she pried them apart.

Elka, Mary, and Rae gathered around. This *had* to be something special. Finally Anna got the wires undone and opened the crate.

"E-e-e-e-e-e-e-h!" screamed Mary, the most excitable of the girls.

There, beautifully laid out on a bed of greens, were what looked to the girls like a lot of dead babies. Mary said so. Anna slammed down the lid of the crate.

"It *can't* be babies," she said.

"Well, I don't want to look again and see what it is," said Mary, still shaken. The others didn't say anything at all.

"Listen, Annale," Elka said, "the man said it would go bad if it wasn't on ice. You can't just forget about it. Open up and look again. Would the Jamisons send us dead babies? Why? What did we ever do to them?"

Anna gingerly approached the crate and looked at it again. When she closed it this time, she turned to them and said: "It would be better if it were babies. You know what it is? Pigs! Thirteen pigs, just in time for *Pesach*. What are we going to do?"

Now the family had real trouble. If Israel found out there had been pigs in the house, they would have to leave the apartment just as it was, leave their clothes, because the presence of the pigs had made everything *trefe*, unclean, unholy. It would be a more complete exodus even than the one they had made from Russia. Something akin to the expulsion from the Garden of Eden. And just before *Pesach*. What could they do?

Suddenly Anna was galvanized into action. "Listen," she said, "for Christians pigs are a great treat, a feast for Easter. Someone must want them. What time will Father be home?"

"He's stopping off at the *shul* tonight. He'll be late. But what's the use? Look at the size of that crate. You're going to take it out in the street and start peddling pigs for Passover? In *this* neighborhood?"

"Don't worry, Mother, I'll take care of it."

"Well, hurry up, pigs are *trefe* enough in this house; spoiled pigs I certainly don't need."

Anna and Mary hurried out of the house. One thing about the Lower East Side: while their few blocks were all Jewish, they didn't have to go very far to get into another world entirely. A few blocks this way, Polish. A few blocks that way, Irish or Italian. They walked until they came to a butcher with strings of pork sausage hanging in his window. Then they went in.

"Listen," said Anna to the man behind the counter, "could you use a pig for Easter? A friend of mine on a farm sent me beautiful pigs, and we don't know how to cook them. Could you use them?"

"Big pigs or little pigs?" asked the butcher.

"I don't know," said Anna. "Pigs."

"Hey, Joe," yelled the butcher to someone inside, "do we need any more pigs for Easter?"

The answer from the back was totally unintelligible, but it must have been affirmative, because the butcher started untying his apron. "Okay, come out here and take over the front; I'm going out for a minute."

"You know, girls," said the butcher, walking with them quickly up the block, "there's nothing easier to cook than roast pig. Put it in the oven and it just about cooks itself." The two girls couldn't think of anything to say.

They crossed the street and walked up the stairs to their apartment. The butcher followed along, still making polite conversation about how to cook pigs. Finally they got to the offending crate. The butcher looked at it disappointedly, noting how huge it was. "Oh," he said, "a big one . . . well . . ."

Then Anna opened up the crate. He was beside himself. "Oh, look at the beauties . . . suckling pigs! Do you know how long it's been since I saw suckling pigs like this? Thirteen of them. What beauties!" Suddenly he seemed to remember he was a businessman and a butcher. His rhapsodies died. "Yes, I suppose I could use them. Can you get me any more?" His eagerness was ill-concealed. He had the attitude of an art connoisseur in front of a hitherto undiscovered Giotto. "Can you get me more?"

"I certainly hope not," said Anna, suddenly envisioning a deluge of little pigs.

"Well, for these I couldn't give you more than . . ." The butcher paused; he looked around. Some innate shrewdness of Elka's made her look bored rather than eager. "I couldn't give you more than fifty dollars." The silence was profound. As one, they looked at one another. No question about it, the *goyim* were mad. Fifty dollars for pigs! And Rae made only ten dollars a week, fourteen hours a day, six days a week.

Anna was the first to recover. "All right. But you have to take them right now. Otherwise they'll spoil. We don't want them to spoil here in the house. You take them with you." The butcher, a big man, started to remonstrate. It was a very heavy crate. "Fifty dollars and you take them with you now or we go to another butcher." Anna was relentless.

"All right. I guess I can manage. But in a minute I could get my cart and it would be so easy. In a minute these pigs won't spoil."

Elka chimed in, in Yiddish, "The man from the farm said keep them on ice or they spoil." Even if the butcher didn't understand her, he understood the finality of her tones.

"Okay, okay, I'm taking them." And he leaned down and lifted the huge crate up, sliding it along his back.

"Where's the fifty dollars?" asked Anna, glad the pigs were leaving the apartment before Israel could see them.

"You'll have to come with me."

So Anna and Mary made a return trip to the butcher store, helping the butcher keep the crate balanced. There they saw the last of the suckling pigs and received a Passover fortune, fifty beautiful dollars.

The girls hurried back to the apartment. They consulted

with Elka. Could they have Passover in that apartment? Could they not tell Israel about it? Elka had the last word. "Listen," she said, "what God and your father don't know won't hurt them. A lie you must never tell. But the truth, who's forcing it out of you?"

It was an especially happy Passover, with a great many little treats that they had never been able to afford before, and Elka had a big sum put away for emergencies. But Anna knew it couldn't end this simply, and she was right. For the rest of that year they had to live in fear and trembling, because every once in a while, unannounced and completely unwelcome, the butcher came. They feared that someday Israel would hear and understand his call: "Hey, girls, you got any more of those beautiful pigs for me?"

Anna Makes Good

ANNA SAILED THROUGH Cornell with colors and long hair flying, a junior year Phi Bete. She was graduated from medical school in 1916.

Diminutive—she never did get taller than four foot ten—pretty and bright, she was an ultrafeminine success in a man's world. And she had the proposals to prove it. More than one doctor had held out a job in his hospital or clinic as bait for marrying him. Anna turned them all down so charmingly, it took weeks for them to realize it.

The only job she wanted was house physician on the Bellevue Fourth Service, Dr. Nammack's medical service. Dr. Nammack told her he had never had a woman on his service and never intended to. Anna qualified for this signal honor in a competitive examination, listened politely to all Dr. Nammack's reasons why she should go somewhere else, and then quietly proceeded to take on the job.

The first thing that happened when Anna began her house physicianship was that she was assigned—as were all interns—an orderly. The orderly was supposed to do the "dirty work"—cleaning up, heavy lifting, all the chores Dr. Nammack had assured Anna she could not do. Anna's orderly was exceptionally large, well over six feet. Unlike most male intern's orderlies, he was also exceptionally uncooperative. Quite obviously he had been told to do nothing but stand there and not follow her orders.

After she had asked him to do a simple chore six times and it hadn't been done, Anna understood. She said nothing and complained to no one. All she would get for complaining would have been a smug "I told you so."

She simply did all her work and all the orderly's chores, too. She was apparently unconcerned as she mopped up blood or grabbed a pail from the orderly to catch some medical debris with. The man followed her around stolidly for two weeks. On a day when she had had no sleep at all the night before, and faced a particularly loathsome mopping-up job, he grabbed the mop and pail out of her hands.

"You go sit down," he said gruffly. "This I do. I can stand no more, and I think you can stand anything!" After that, she never had any more orderly trouble.

After two months Dr. Nammack asked her in, called her down for insisting on working where she wasn't wanted, and then told her she was the best house physician he'd ever had.

Dr. Nammack was very fond of making a joke—especially if the joke was at the expense of some of his underlings. No one was fonder of pricking the balloon of pretension than Dr. Nammack. One day, he must have felt that Anna was overreaching herself and he should take her down a peg. To do it, he chose an oft-used jest that had discomfited many a male intern. He was sure it would do the trick with a mere female.

"Dr. Kleegman," he said as he was making his rounds with all the interns in tow, "would you explain to us the reason that most babies are born at night?" He expected Anna to attempt a learned and quite unsubstantiated scientific opinion involving the phases of the moon, the pull of the tides, and the splitting of the atom. Anna Kleegman was not that easily discombobulated. "Certainly I can explain it, Doctor," she replied, "it's because so many babies are born nine months to the minute after they are conceived."

After that, Dr. Nammack, at least in public, confined himself to asking completely scientific opinions from Anna Kleegman.

One of Anna's chores while she was house physician on Dr. Nammack's service was to arbitrate the great Pneumonia War. At that time, pneumonia was the Number One Killer in America, and everybody thought he had discovered "the" cure. Dr. Nammack was testing a combination of whiskey and *nux vomica*, a form of strychnine. He was convinced of its curative powers, and since the dosage was two ounces of whiskey four times a day, so were his patients. Indeed, it was the ambition of every Bowery bum to contract pneumonia and be sent off to Bellevue.

An influential visiting physician on Anna's service—who was also a teetotaler—was horrified by the treatment. He felt it had no medical validity at all, and was attracting a very low level of patient. He wanted to try a serum, developed in Canada, which, he believed, would abolish pneumonia altogether.

He acquired a considerable amount of the serum and got hold of Anna. "Dr. Kleegman, as a doctor and as a woman," he said to her, "you cannot approve of Dr. Nammack's treatment."

Anna, who was already administering Dr. Nammack's "cure" and did indeed find it a nuisance, not only because the patients got high, but because the strychnine made them terribly sick, was more than willing to test another method.

She agreed eagerly. "I'll do it, provided neither you nor Dr. Nammack interferes with my pneumonia cases for the next month."

And for a month she carefully divided her pneumonia cases into three parts like all Gaul—one part—the happy cases—received their tots of whiskey and *nux vomica*. One part received the vaccine, somewhat disconsolately but, in the main, philosophically. Bellevue patients had experience being losers. And the third group received a placebo, being kept, as in all good scientific experiments, as a control group.

The control group showed a significantly higher degree of recoveries than either of the test groups—proving that rest, fluids, sympathy, and freedom from medicine at least didn't interfere with the patient curing himself. Thus Anna negotiated the peace treaty in the Great Pneumonia War.

From her intern's quarters to the new apartment at 115th Street was a half-hour ride on the subway. Anna often rode at very odd hours of the night—particularly if her conscientiousness had kept her long after intern's hours at the side of a deathbed or at the wrist of a patient in crisis until death or life had won the decision.

But as often as she could Anna came home to the apartment. After all, no matter how involved she was with her doctoring, home was home. Her late night rides put her in contact with whatever seamy New Yorkers she did not meet as patients in the hospital. Ever a pushover for a hard-luck story, she was forever giving out advice, medical counsel, and what little money she had to fellow subway riders. Finally Elka, who felt that too much of Anna's meager spending money was being passed on to the subway nogoodniks, told her: "Listen, they are just poisoning themselves with more drink if you give them money. Bring them home; I'll give them a good meal. Then you'll know they get fed."

Of course, this was all the encouragement Anna needed. From then on, she brought home one or another subway pickup every time she came. Very often these derelicts were pitifully grateful for the meal they got, so grateful that there could be no question of sending them out again into the cold. Hospitality demanded they be given a bed. But in an apartment where every bed was occupied, the putting up of a guest presented a problem. It was not a problem for long. Sophie was the youngest; she would give up her bed—after all, a youngster could sleep anywhere. And that was where Sophie slept . . . anywhere—usually, on a quilt spread out on the kitchen table, in spite of Sophie's protests that she was the worst sleeper in the bunch.

One night Anna picked up an unfortunate just as she left the hospital. She took her home, fed her, put her to bed, and moved a protesting Sophie to the kitchen table.

"But, Anna," groaned Sophie, "I have to take a final exam tomorrow. I won't sleep a wink and I'll get a terrible mark."

"Nonsense," said Anna, "just close your eyes and breathe deeply. There's nothing easier than going to sleep." This was said with the fervor of a busy house physician who hadn't closed her eyes for the last thirty-six hours and who could have gone to sleep in the kitchen sink if she had to. Beyond muttering grumpily to herself, Sophie made no further protest.

She made no further protest, that is, until their guest for the night suddenly appeared in the kitchen. Sophie, still wide awake, watched in horror as the woman opened the drawer of the cabinet and took out a long carving knife. Sophie screamed at the top of her lungs as the woman, holding the knife in a businesslike position, headed back into the rest of the apartment where Anna, Mary, Rachel, Elka, and Israel were sleeping. Not unnaturally, this made the lunatic pay some attention to Sophie. Sophie hopped off the kitchen table and kept it between herself and the knife. "Stay still," said the lunatic. "Why would I hurt you?" This question would have seemed a lot more reasonable if she weren't by then chasing Sophie around the table, knife at the ready. Sophie's screams brought the rest of the family tumbling into the kitchen. The lunatic was speedily disarmed, seemed genuinely chagrined at having committed a social solecism, admitted that she had these fits sometimes, and prepared to take her leave.

Anna gently but firmly said that she was on her way back to Bellevue and thought the woman should come with her. The lunatic pleasantly agreed. "I don't understand why they let me out," she said. "After all, I kept telling them I was crazy."

Anna arranged for the permanent placement of her overnight guest in a treatment center, then once again went home. This time she refrained from picking up anyone on the way.

She walked into the house just as Sophie was leaving for school. "I'm awfully sorry, honey," said Anna. "Do well on your exams." Sophie didn't dignify this remark with an answer. Elka had forbidden her to worry Anna about the contretemps of the night before, but Sophie couldn't resist saying as she walked out, "Next time you can sleep on the kitchen table—you show *me* how easy it is."

Anna apologized to Elka. "Well," said Elka, "it's not your fault exactly. You're not learning to be a doctor to *meshugenahs* and crazy people. But from now on, we have a rule. Hannahle, you hear me; it's an absolute rule. Sophie has to have her sleep, and so do you. I can't have either of you running around all night by the kitchen table. From now on you bring them home to dinner—yes. But no more sleeping by strangers in this house."

At that point, Anna's subway excursions finished anyway. The family fortunes had taken yet another nose dive, and Anna took to walking the hundred blocks between Bellevue and the apartment just to save money.

Mary wasn't working, but she had found a steady fellow, who was bringing in the munificent sum of seventy-five dollars a week as a foreman. When Mary's union activities got him fired, it was total disaster. Elka decided the family should go into its own business. Then Mary could get married, be as sympathetic with unions as she liked, and still bring in money.

Anna went unhappily to Dr. Nammack. "I'm going to have to leave the hospital." Nammack looked her over and asked, "Are you pregnant?"

"I'm not even married," she replied.

If he thought this was a non sequitur he didn't mention it. When she explained the financial problems of her family, he went to the Bellevue Board of Governors. And that august fellowship put up five hundred dollars for a bagel-and-lox store. Mary and Harry promptly got married. The business soon was doing so well that it employed both Elka and Israel. Rae kept on doggedly stitching garments by the piece, and the family fortunes rose again.

Mother and the Ambulance

As AN INTERN and resident, Anna, like all the doctors, rode the ambulance as a part of her regular duties. If there was no patient inside, the doctor could ride in comfort in the back of the van. But if a patient occupied the bunk, the doctor had to stand on a narrow ledge under the open door, like a fireman, holding on for dear life to an outside handle while giving the necessary emergency care en route.

One day, early in her Bellevue internship, Anna was riding the ambulance with a patient who was about to give birth. Anna, already a veteran of ten deliveries, saw clearly that this one was in the earliest stages and was likely to go on until the whole hospital was sick of it. She had told the driver that there was no real hurry and that he could take it easy, and they were jolting along at a spanking 1916 pace when a big bump threw the ambulance into a sickly swerve. Anna, thinking first of her patient, put out both hands to keep the pregnant woman from falling out of the narrow bunk. At the same time, the driver pulled hard on the steering wheel to get the ambulance back on course. The result was inevitable. Anna fell off into the middle of a cobblestone street. While her whole past ran in front of her eyes, her feet ran up the street.

The astonished driver looked out his windshield and suddenly clomped on his brakes. There, *in front* of the ambulance, stood Anna, waving her arms in a frantic semaphore. The ambulance stopped at her skirts, barely avoiding a new medical emergency.

"How the—excuse me—did you get there?" said the driver, who had been going a smart twenty miles an hour.

"I ran," said Anna.

Needless to say this incident made her firm friends with the driver, who had great admiration for her sprinting powers. The next time they were called out together for an emergency, he proceeded at an extremely decorous rate, just in case she should have to jog again. The call had been for a man having a fit, and when the ambulance arrived, Anna jumped out, ready to administer medicines, hold down his tongue, and do everything fitting to the occasion. In the building lobby she found a rather large woman berating a small man who sat disconsolately in a lobby armchair and seemed to shrink with each new onslaught of her tongue.

Anna said cheerily: "I'm the doctor with the ambulance. Do you know where the emergency case is?"

"Please, Doctor," said the little man.

"Yes," interrupted the belligerent woman, "he's right there. *I* called the ambulance for him, and about time you got here, too."

"Well," said Anna, "he seems to have recovered nicely. What kind of fit was it, and how do you feel now, sir?"

"Please, Doctor," said the little man.

"Recovered, nothing," interrupted the bellicose lady, "he's right in the middle of it. Look at him. We're supposed to go to my mother's, and he absolutely won't. He's having a fit . . . a fit of stubbornness!"

Not all emergencies were destined to end so absurdly. Another time Anna and the ambulance answered a call for an attempted suicide. When Anna arrived she found a fragilely lovely young girl at the point of death. Immediate measures revived her slightly, but what actually saved her life was the fact that the poison she had swallowed was shoe dye so strong she had vomited most of it up before it could be absorbed.

The ambulance speeded her back to the hospital, where Anna acted quickly to save her life, pumped out her stomach, and stayed by her bed until it was apparent she would survive.

The next day Anna paid a visit to the prison ward (if you fail at suicide you have committed a crime) to see the girl and find out what had made her so desperate. After all, Anna had saved a life and she did not want to see it taken again.

"What made you do it, dear?" asked Anna in a very motherly fashion. She may have been two years older than the girl herself.

"I swore I tell nobody ever," said the girl, her lips, quivering. "But you are a woman, and not old. You maybe will understand."

"Of course. I'll try and help. Tell me, please."

"I came here alone to make money to bring all the family," said the girl. "But I am the first. The only one from the family, from even the willage. I know no persons here, and none knows me. Then I meet a nice boy. Wery a nice boy. Handsome, someone like my own. He likes me. He valks me from vork. Every evening he comes. Ve talk, no more. I know how a girl alone must do. I do nothing wrong. Still, it's good to valk with someone. Then he doesn't come one night, not the next. It's three weeks, and I vorry. Yesterday, he come again. He see me. He say he can't vork so hard and he can't be poor. He is to marry a rich girl with a father with a good business and a fine job. I say all right and I vant to say a nice good-bye, vish him good luck. But he didn't ewen stay. He left me right there in the middle street. And when he treated me like that, not like a lady, but like you know how, nothing, my heart was so squeezed, I couldn't live no more.

"So I went to the drugstore and I bought the vorst bottle, the one printed 'danger' and 'poison,' and I swallowed all.

"But it didn't make me die. It only made me womit."

"Poor girl, poor, poor girl," said Anna. "Don't worry. I'll do something. Would you like to come home with me? I have young sisters, and there are always lots of people around. If I can arrange it, do you want to come?" And, inevitably, once the girl was wrested from the arms of the law, Anna delivered her into the arms of an eager fellow countryman looking for a wife. If Anna never mentioned the girl's suicide, she also never mentioned the boy's fiancée in the Old Country. After all, a girl in the hand was better than beating the bushes.

When Anna finished her training and became a full-fledged practicing physician, she celebrated by joining the army. At the special request of Surgeon-General Gorgas—the yellow-fever hero—she became a contract surgeon during the First World War.

At the end of the war, when she was all of twenty-four, she was appointed a full professor at Greensboro College for Women, in North Carolina. She returned to New York in 1919, and went into private practice, becoming a surgeon on the staff of The Hospital for Special Surgery and The New York Infirmary, a successful gynecologist, obstetrician, a "joiner" who generally wound up president of many women's groups, a lecturer very much in demand, a founding fellow of the American College of Obstetrics and Gynecology, one of the earliest members of the American Society of Marriage Counselors, a vice-president of the New York Women's Medical Association, and the author of articles and books on contraception, the prevention of venereal disease, marriage counseling, and *The Mature Woman*. So few women were willing to admit they were mature, that the paperback publishers reverted to her original title—*It's Never Too Late to Love*.

Mother and Maurice

Which brings us to love, and to Anna, love meant Maurice. He was one of the boarders on the Jamison farm, and while he had partaken of the memorable Thanksgiving dinner it had not then moved *him* to a proposal. In fact, he seemed to follow Anna around only to disapprove of her.

One winter vacation while she was still in college, Anna was at the farm with Sarah Jamison and a happy group of young men and women. They were all sleigh-riding down the hill in back of the farm. First the boys and girls kept to strictly segregated sleds. Then a few of the more adventurous girls began to ride with the boys, and pretty soon they were all belly-whopping together, a very daring activity in those days.

As Anna ran up the hill, she heard a deep voice call, "Here, Anna Kleegman, come here." She turned and saw a sled ready to go, although she couldn't see who was riding it, with his face turned down the hill. She ran up, hopped on, and away they glided, with her arms holding him tightly. As they gathered speed, the sled took a sharp swerve and they both rolled off into the snow. Anna rose giggling, trying to brush off the snow and disentangle her long skirts at the same time. To her surprise, the driver of the sled was the tall, handsome young man who had always seemed to disapprove of her. He wasn't laugh-

ing at their fall at all. In fact, he seemed rather scornful of all
the merrymaking.

He looked at Anna. He looked unhappy. And that was all
she needed. Her heart went out to him at that moment. In
some ways, it never came back.

Anna said to him anxiously, "Did you hurt yourself when
you fell off the sled?"

"No," he replied, looking sadder still.

"Good," said Anna, feeling free to return to her laughter.

"Anna Kleegman, why do you laugh so much? What do you
find so funny about life?"

"Why, everything," said Anna, not stopping to think. "The
snow and the sleigh-riding, and coming to the farm, and going
to college. In America, life is wonderful. Where did you come
from?"

"Poland."

"And isn't life here so much better? Why aren't you happy
. . . oh, what *is* your name?"

"My name is Maurice, Maurice Daniels. And if I were to
start now telling you all the reasons I'm sad, we could stay here
until tomorrow and I wouldn't be finished. When I'm so full
of sorrow, how can you be so full of fun?" She saw that he said
that wistfully. How much he, too, wanted to be full of fun. She
started laughing at him, and picked up a big chunk of snow.
After all, they were both young. It was a wonderful afternoon,
and she could make him laugh, too, if she tried hard enough.

After that, the general fun always seemed to wind up with
Anna and Maurice together. She learned a little more about
him. He had first come to America to Dayton, Ohio, where
he'd built up a little store that he had sold for the munificent
sum of five hundred dollars. It was no small achievement for a
newly arrived greenhorn. He had sewn his savings into his
clothes and come to New York to make his fortune, but had
only been in the city a few days before he was talked out of his
entire savings in a phony stock deal.

Now he was boarding at the farm and selling portraits door to door for a company that made original oil paintings, painted by hand, from the customer's favorite photograph.

Anna didn't think this was a good profession for a nice Jewish boy, particularly not for one who might become her husband. They began talking of futures. Maurice told her one of his great disappointments was that in Poland he had been a prize student, while here he was a failing businessman. In America, it was his great ambition to get back to school.

"Well," said Anna, "if what you want to do is go back to school, why are you staying in a job where you make just enough to buy water for your oatmeal? You are starving here. In a couple of years, I will be going to New York. Why not go there now and establish yourself? You can starve there just as well as here."

"But," protested Maurice, "how can I study, if I haven't enough money even to eat?"

"In New York," said Anna, "you can study free, free of charge. It doesn't cost anything. You are an educated man. It's a crime to throw yourself away here."

The argument was ended two years later, when Maurice asked, "If I go, Anna, can I go with you? And if I study, will you marry me?" Maurice moved to New York. The answer to him, as Anna's answer always was to him: Yes.

Mary and Harry were making a real go of the delicatessen store and were full of the joys of married life. After having emerged triumphantly from his course at a Maryland college, Maurice decided to join the army. Anna thought he might be killed, he might be maimed, he might meet a mademoiselle. War was hell; marriage was bliss. So on September 6, 1918, Maurice was inducted into the army, and on September 12 Anna Kleegman and Maurice Blumberg Daniels were married. In order to pay for the license, they had to pool their joint resources. He had a dollar. She had a dollar and ten cents. It was just enough for the marriage license and the subway to Far Rockaway. He wore his brand-new army uniform; she wore white—surgical whites. The subway ride took them to the one-room beach bungalow where Elka, Mary, and Harry and the two other girls were staying. Israel moved the family out to the neighbors' to give Anna and Maurice a six-day honeymoon. But since the neighbor could only offer meals and not beds, it was a much-kibitzed, much-interrupted honeymoon.

Before Maurice got out of Maryland, the war was over.

Now Maurice and Anna could plan the future.

"I think I'll be a doctor," said Maurice. "We'll practice together. I'll be an obstetrician and you'll be a pediatrician."

"Well," said Anna, "that's a nice idea. But is it really practical? Look at it this way. The Daniels family already has a doctor. We need a lawyer. It's a fine profession, and just right for you. You can talk anyone into anything. You're a wonderful talker. I can sit and listen to you for hours. And being a lawyer is all talk."

This description of his future profession so enchanted Maurice that he enrolled in New York University Law School and stayed for two years, supported, as was the rest of the family, by Anna's earnings and the bagel-and-lox store. Then he met an up-and-coming real-estate magnate who instantly recognized his talents. Boy, *could* Maurice talk! And Maurice was offered an incredible salary to go into real estate: $150 a week. He left his schooling without a backward glance.

To the humdrum business of real estate and insurance he brought the foresight and imagination of a visionary. He wrote a book called *Eat Your Cake and Have It,* which outlined the major ideas of what was to become the FHA program. And he also began one of the very first medical-insurance programs.

When Maurice moved on to his own real-estate and insurance business, it was successful from the beginning. Anna and Maurice became the nucleus of a very large family.

They provided housing, advice, and financing for all the Kleegmans. And they started enthusiastically on a family of their own and had their first girl, Dorothea. That was fine; it didn't matter that the first child was a girl because they were going to have lots more. When Miriam was born a year and a half later, it was a little less delightful. Maurice definitely wanted a *boy*. But they'd have more, many more children.

Meanwhile Rae, the quiet Kleegman, came home with a matrimonially inclined gentleman caller. And what a caller! The family still talks about his beauty in hushed tones. He was never referred to by name, but only as Rae's handsome husband. Maurice, impressed by his looks and his ambition for doing great things, took him into the business, a business that was thriving beyond anyone's wildest dreams. But it soon became obvious that Rae's husband was suited only for Maurice's job as president of the company.

So Maurice set him up in a business of his own, selling cars. Rae, who had quietly assessed the situation herself and taken a nursing course once she was relieved of the necessity of supporting the family, went back to work.

Maurice discovered the stock exchange. The greenhorn who had lost his whole savings on a phony stock deal became the seasoned investor who bought on margin and made killing after killing on the market.

Mimmi and Thea remember clearly one day when he came home carrying an enormous sack, like Santa Claus. Only, it was on a brightly lit sunny summer beach day.

"Come here, girls," he said, jingling the sack. "Come here and see this." He counted 10,000 brand-new, bright copper pennies, dividing them equally. "That's how many dollars I made on the stock exchange today."

During the twenties everyone was a tycoon, but Maurice

was more of a tycoon than most. He had a great family (and it was going to get bigger; it was 1927, and another was on the way). He had a great business. He and Anna had marvelous friends. The future looked great. And *this* child was going to be a boy.

In 1928 I was born and I was a girl. In 1929 the stock market also failed to live up to Maurice's expectations.

Although everyone was going broke paying off ten cents on the dollar, Maurice could not bring himself to do that. His investors were all friends. He had promised to make money for them. The stock market might disappoint them, but he couldn't. Grimly, he bankrupted himself by not going into bankruptcy—and paid off one hundred cents on every dollar he owed. Anna and Maurice didn't mind being poor again. After all, no one had any money. The only real casualty of the crash was Rae's husband. He put his hat on one morning and walked out. No one ever heard from him again.

In the thirties and forties the relationship between Maurice and Anna fluctuated much more widely than the stock market, which for as long as Maurice continued speculating in it, stayed depressingly down.

Two volatile, hardheaded people, they couldn't be together for a minute without finding something to argue over. But when they tried separation, it brought them running back to each other's arms. They were two complete individualists who had only to see each other to become more individualistic than ever.

There was no question that they loved each other. There was never indifference between them. But it was impossible for them to live together or apart.

Anna's practice evolved from obstetrics and gynecology to straight gynecology, to menopausal gynecology, and then to marriage counseling. She would have liked very much to be able to give herself wise counsel, instead of seesawing from estrangement to reconciliation.

Finally, She Is My Mother!

AND WHAT KIND of person is she, now that she moves into actual memory and I really know her? Unique, with an unmistakable panache, funny, loving, and the best friend of everyone who knew her. Part of her success as a doctor came from how little she looked the part. Every inch of her four foot ten seemed to be in motion all the time. She never walked anywhere but ran, ran, ran to get where she was going. Her voice, especially her laughter, preceded her at a party or down hospital halls, as she dashed to catch up with it. Lively and vivacious, she worked an incredible schedule, and then would happily dance all night through. How she loved dancing! And when she wore out partner after partner, she would sit down and sing old Russian songs until the sun rose. Her sleep was caught in catnaps, which she was perfectly capable of taking right in front of you, if the party got dull or the lecture was uninspiring.

Her clothes were indescribable. No self-respecting charlady would have worn them, but Mother carried them off with aplomb. She dressed in whatever came to hand—and since all her new clothes were put away as too good—her wardrobe had a vintage, costumey look, enhanced by a totally feminine love of frills and furbelows applied in profusion, to cover holes, darns and ineradicable spots. These decorations were chosen totally without regard to the color or cut of the dress they bedecked. The result was true "camp," a bit before its time, but so outrageous as to often achieve true style.

Although she never wore high-heeled shoes, she collected them, and her closet was filled with pairs from the most expensive Fifth Avenue stores. Her usual footgear was open sandals with as few straps as possible, and an uncompromisingly flat heel. In the winter she paid homage to the inclement weather by covering them with a pair of transparent overshoes (for dress) or men's galoshes (for everyday).

Her other extravagance was a passion for secondhand furs. Long before the craze for "amusing little fun" fur coats, Mother collected outré animals. She collected not only furs but furriers. And whenever she found a new one, we all got our share. We were a walking Ritz Thrift Shop from the time we were old enough to walk.

Mother herself would then acquire a quite splendid wrap, which might have seen better days, but still had a lot of chic left. An elegant mink covered a slew of sartorial sins (who can tell a second- or third-hand mink?)

Since Mother often had as many as five or six disreputable fur coats hanging in her closet, I wasn't terribly surprised when a lady came up to me one day and said: "Oh, you're Dr. Daniels' daughter. Your mother is the most remarkable woman." She went on to tell a story about her first consultation with my mother. Her husband was out of a job and she had no coat, even though it was bitter cold. So Mother went straight to her own closet and took out a Persian-lamb jacket she had just got that week. She handed it over to the patient, and the astonished woman wore it all winter. "Imagine," this enthusiast for Mother's generosity exclaimed, "Persian lamb!"

I could well imagine the Persian lamb, because after the

grateful lady had returned it, I inherited it. She had consulted my mother for an advanced case of pregnancy. The jacket fit her. But a garment less suited to a skinny twelve-year-old I can't conjure. It was black; it was voluminous; and it was more Mede than Persian. However, to this day Mother's delighted "I've found a marvelous new furrier" means for all the family's females a downpour of shrugs, boas, stoles, three-quarter coats, and full-length wraps.

Her gaiety, wit, and brilliance, and her unfailing kindness to people in trouble, attracted a coterie of exciting, neurotic, extraordinary people. Many of them were in the theater.

Maurice was a host with the bravura camaraderie that plays so well with theater people. With or without money, he managed to create a welcome so warm every guest came back for more.

And one thing Mother insisted on. Her children always made the scene with her. A famous director would be regaled with our dramatic readings of "Shandu the Magician." And our rendition of "I'll give to you a paper of pins" in song and pantomime was an off-Broadway *succès fou,* although it suffered terribly from the fact that there wasn't a boy in the family to play the rejected suitor.

Of the three of us, Thea was the bright one, Mimmi was the pretty one, and I was the baby. These categories were not mutually exclusive. Thea was voted one of the three most popular freshmen in her class at Cornell, and Mimmi had a college record of straight A's. I had another distinction. I was going to be the doctor. From the time when I was five, and held a playmate's head together so that Mother could stitch it (after he had split his skull open on a radiator), my scientific abilities were unquestioned.

Mother started taking me along with her on her rounds.

She had a huge charity practice, although in those depression years money was a thing she spent but never had. She would often send a paying patient to someone else because she simply didn't have the time to see her. But she never turned away a patient who couldn't pay.

We would climb innumerable stairs in innumerable tenements, and if I expressed surprise or distaste at the way some of her patients lived, she would say to me: "It was much worse, what we came from in Borschevka. Don't forget that. And don't forget that it is your responsibility to see that people should not have to live like this. Make a world where no one is hungry. I'm trying to make one where no one is sick."

Her crusading spirit was not confined to sickness. As a doctor to the very unfortunate, first at the New York State Training School for Girls and then at the House of Detention for Women, time and again she pleaded with anyone who would listen for some kind of useful rehabilitation program, and for something to relieve the stark boredom of prison. Although the methods she proposed in the thirties seem the merest common sense today, she was accused of coddling prisoners and not understanding the problems.

She was also a fervent crusader for the right of women to plan families, and was a medical director of one of the Planned Parenthood clinics. Her frequent claim, and one that is still true today, is that the rich can plan families. It is only the poor who are denied the privileges of contraception.

Another crusade of hers for yet another underprivileged group was what was called in the family her "sex after sixty syndrome." She was a firm believer that the golden years would be a lot more golden if the postmenopausal women didn't think their sex life had ended. In the thirties, you have no idea what a shocking idea this was . . . enough to get her virtually ostracized in the best circles, where she would insist on making this subject dinner conversation.

But in fact the very best circles came to her. Young, gay, and frantic—the Daniels' parties were attended by what seemed to us "all New York." Even in the depression when money was as short in our house as it was everywhere else, our grocery bills were astronomical. Still guests never had enough to eat; there were just too many unexpected droppers-in.

But everyone was very gay. Anna was the gayest of all. All her theatrical friends told her she could revive any show just be being in the audience, she enjoyed it all so much.

One night, one of her friends, a producer of hit musicals, brought in a microphone, blank records, and a bulky recording device that he hid behind the couch. Then he started telling her funny stories, recording her reactions. The resulting records were half an hour of Anna's unrestrained laughter. At first he played them at parties simply to set a mood. Then he began using them as background for backer's auditions. Anna became the first laugh track.

Even those friends who weren't associated with the theater tended to have children who were. Sonny Fogg was one of mother's good friends at Cornell. She came to mother very distressed because her son wanted to be an actor. Mother, of course, told her what a wonderful field it was, how stimulating and exciting and filled with opportunity—as, of course, it proved to be for Sonny's son, Montgomery Clift. And the nice little son of friends "who's just your age" and whom I avoided like the plague was Stuart Whitman.

One of Mother's patients was Lou Tellegen, who had been SarahBernhardt's leading man and ever since tried to make people aware of what a matinee idol he was on his own.

Lou was a marvelously handsome man who had posed for Rodin's statue *The Kiss*. He was very attractive to women, and happily married to quite a few of them. Among other things that Mother had treated him for were burns he suffered when he fell asleep while smoking. The burns had required seventy-two skin grafts, and, even so, there were a few bad scars. Lou was very fond of entering a room with Mother, attracting everyone's attention—something he did easily—and saying, "I want you to meet the only woman who ever left her mark on me . . . Anna Daniels—and here it is!" At that point he'd unbutton his shirt and show off his beautiful skin grafts!

Other theater people in the crowd were Jay Gorney and Yip Harburg—their hit song "Brother, Can You Spare a Dime?" was the theme song of the depression, and Yip went on to write great shows like *Finian's Rainbow*—and Audrey Wood and Billy Liebling, the famous play and actor's agents.

I doubt that Mother, especially during that period when the theater was thriving creatively but not financially, ever paid for a ticket to anything. And I know that my sisters and I sat through endless turgid proletarian dramas, as well as the greatest theater of the thirties, simply because Mother had tickets (free, of course) and *somebody* had to use them. Suitability of subject never bothered her. Her theory was that if it was a play it was good for the children. (The end result of this is that I can always be prevailed upon to go see anything as long as the curtain goes up on it. And none of the avantest avant-garde theater of today or the offest off-off-Broadway seems nearly as wild to me as the things I saw when I was six or seven years old. Probably none of it is.)

Weekends at the beach house would be filled with lots of lively people, making merry. And I still remember, as the epitome of desolation, the desertion of Sunday nights, when everyone would wend their feckless way to the city—leaving us in what seemed a virtually uninhabited house.

The one person who was always there, besides the staff, was Mother. She might work until all hours of the night—and of course she did. She might have to operate at six thirty in the morning. But her valiant little car would arrive—perhaps long after we had all given up and gone to sleep—and leave, certainly long before we ever had to get up. Still, she had spent her night with us. And there was always that delightfully hazy memory of the last thing at night when she had come in and kissed us good night, and the first thing in the morning, a barely remembered Hello. We knew that if we needed her, we could stay up late or get up early. She was there.

Mother and the Whippet

WHILE ANNA was the only person I ever knew who could be accused of jay-driving, and who had many cars, the one most associated with her by anyone unfortunate enough to ride in it was her Whippet.

It had been left to her in Lou Tellegen's will, to pay off his doctor's bills, and was an ideal car for an idol of the stage and screen—long, lean, capable of speeds up to 120 miles per hour—and made to seat, in a pinch, two people who were very fond of each other.

For Anna, who never went anywhere unless accompanied by at least three or four other people, and who never drove above twenty miles an hour unless she had a hospital emergency, it was remarkably unsuitable. On the other hand, her driving, when she got behind the wheel of the Whippet, did take on a Hyde-like terror. She knew it was a car designed for speed, and it made her assume a don't-spare-the-horses insouciance.

She would start out with maybe one passenger to a very specific destination. As she was leaving the house, she would see someone on the street, headed for a bus or some other safe and secure form of public transportation. "Hello, Mr. Smith," she'd call. "Where are you headed? Can't I drop you?"

If Mr. Smith had never before been offered this invitation he might reply unwarily, "Oh, that's all right, Doctor, I'm just going to the station." If he had ever been picked up by her before and he was a quick thinker, he replied, "No, Doctor, I'm just going right back in the house. I've noticed my ivy needs trimming and I'm going to stay right here and do it."

The hapless pedestrian would wind up on the lap of another passenger, with Anna assuring him his destination—station, house, or heaven—was right on the way.

Anna would then step on the gas, rolling along happily at twenty miles an hour. She had, however, got her driver's license early in the twenties when traffic laws were free and easy and one took traffic lights with a grain of salt.

"Dr. Daniels," a passenger would shout, "you just went right through a red light!"

"Oh, no," my mother would reply, "that's perfectly all right. I made a right turn on that light. That's legal."

"No, it isn't, Doctor."

"It isn't? Well, it certainly was when I got my license." And on she'd drive.

If the passengers were lucky, she might not see a hitchhiker for three or four blocks, and they would ride along in comparative comfort. When she did spot a hitchhiker, she invariably stopped.

"Where in heaven's name are you going to put him?" the agonized passenger at the bottom of the pile would ask.

"Oh, don't worry, there's plenty of room," was Anna's invariable reply. And there always was plenty of room. Passengers filled the front, the trunk, the running boards, and on a day when the hitchhiking was heavy, even the hood.

The Whippet sometimes limped along under the weight of as many as twelve passengers. And should anyone intentionally leave the car before their announced destination, Mother would stop, back up, and say sternly: "Now, I'm going right *there*. You get back on!"

On the other hand, on a bad or bumpy road she would strew passengers without being aware of it.

One day, by picking up a number of total strangers, she had loaded the car rather more heavily than usual. Her announced trip was from the beach house to the city, and she had made four detours to let her passengers off. She was down to a fairly manageable three passengers, two in front, sitting one on top of the other, and one sitting with his feet hanging out of the trunk.

She got off the Queensboro Bridge, proceeded to Fifth Avenue and Fifty-seventh Street, and made an illegal left turn. Just as she turned, the car gave an unmistakable groan and simply stopped dead. No one who had had as much experience with a last breath as Anna could mistake that sound.

Unfortunately, she was in a hurry. She looked up and saw that she was now stopped where she blocked traffic in four directions, directly athwart one of New York's busiest intersections. Three policemen were descending on her.

"Excuse me, sir," she said to the topmost man on her right. "Will you just take this wheel for a moment. I want to see if I can start the car." She picked up her doctor's bag, got out smilingly, and simply walked quietly away. As she looked back at the crowd that converged, she said to her conscience placatingly, "Well, I did have to get to the hospital soon. And after all, I left them my beautiful car!"

Mother and the Radishes

MY MOTHER, who had taught for a year at Greensboro College for Women, was much impressed with the southern belle, and decided that at least one of her daughters should have the soft charm of the land under Mason and Dixon. Obviously, the daughter best suited for the role was my sister Mimmi, who after three months down South was incomprehensible and irresistible in about equal proportions. Mimmi had also acquired in those three months a number of devoted southern gentlemen callers.

One of these gentlemen followed her up to New York, and since she was dated up for every night of her Easter vacation, apparently did so solely for the pleasure of chauffeuring her back. The trip would be a long one, especially since Wally's car was unreliable on hills and the Blue Ridge Mountains were in the way.

Wally had planned to start at six in the morning, showing how little he knew my sister Mimmi. She was, of course, just settling down to a sounder sleep when he rang the doorbell. He rang and rang and finally heard vague sounds of doors unlocking.

"Mimmi?" he boomed hopefully.

"Good morning," said my mother, flinging wide the door.

Wally could not manage an appropriate response in spite of

the indomitable traditions of courtesy in the Old South. Perhaps he was struck dumb by the attire my mother regarded as suitable for answering the doorbell.

She came to the door that morning in what had once been a modest nightgown with high neck and long sleeves. Since she couldn't stand the confinement of either, she had cut the sleeves and the neck away, generously. Nature had added a few more deletions during the five or six years of wear and tear. (If a garment proved comfortable, Anna wore it until it fell off. While she would industriously sew on it to keep it in condition, she always chose whatever color thread was closest at hand, so that it soon became a coat, dress, or gown of many colors.) She had answered the door that morning with more showing than her hospitality.

"Come right in," she said. "Mimmi is almost ready. Wouldn't you like some breakfast before you go?"

Poor Wally must have had visions of bacon, eggs, toast, and coffee, because he accepted the offer eagerly. Since we were all away at school—the girls, that is—and Daddy—in one of the downs of their up-and-down marriage—was once again an absentee parent, Mother was living in an apartment hotel in what was called a four-room suite. It served her as office and home, and was big enough to allow for either her girls or her husband's temporary return. During my school vacations I slept on a couch beside the diathermy machine and under the sunlamp. I was always petrified that I'd turn on a switch in my sleep and either bake or broil to death.

However, for light housekeeping (and Mother's housekeeping was so light as to be virtually airborne) the apartment did contain something Elka referred to in mock Russian as a kitchen-nyet. This was two electric burners, one cupboard, and the kind of half-refrigerator one often finds in office bars.

Mother sped in to wake Mimmi—who took an hour to change her mind, much less her clothes—and then came back to Wally seated at the pull-down kitchen table.

"Let's see what I can offer you," she said. She flung open the refrigerator door, and found it empty. However, shoved way in the back, where they had been abandoned as inedible even by her ravenous daughters, stood a plate with six moldy radishes. The night before, we had all rejected them and insisted on going to the hotel restaurant for sustenance. But Mother was a firm believer in the proverb that a crust eaten with friends is preferable to a banquet alone, and was undaunted.

"Ah," she chortled, rubbing her hands with satisfaction that her cupboard was not totally bare, "radishes!" She took them over to the sink and carefully scrubbed each one, trying in vain to restore them to vibrant redness.

Even Mother noticed the agony of Wally's expression when the dish of radishes was placed squarely in front of him without any other accompaniment. "There," said Anna proudly, with the air of one who has effortlessly whipped up a soufflé for forty-five. Then, encouragingly, "We always love radishes; they're so healthy!"

"Is Mimmi ready?" he asked.

"Oh, yes," said Anna, "she'll be right out. Now, eat up."

Wally looked at the radishes. They looked right back at him. Under Anna's genial eye he picked up a radish and surveyed it from all sides. He turned it over. He threw it up in the air with a touch of bravado, and then, being a gentleman of the old school, he popped it into his mouth.

He looked as though that first bite damn near killed him. But he chewed and chewed and chewed. Perhaps he hoped to be saved by the belle, but Mimmi did not make an appearance. He chewed on long after every dubious vestige had disappeared down his gullet. But at last he had to abandon such an obvious dissimulation.

"Thank you, ma'am; that was delicious," he said. "Now Mimmi and I have got to be goin'."

"Oh, she'll be *right* out. Now, Wally, don't be bashful. Have another radish!"

Mother's affinity for radishes was not a sometime thing. Having survived a childhood in which starvation was the commonest cause of death, lost a fortune during the crash, and lived through a major depression in which her richest patients became charity cases, she was sure of only one thing. She knew where her next meal was coming from . . . from the remains of the last. If she ate at a restaurant, she buttered all the available rolls, wrapped them in the most voluminous cloth napkin (if the restaurant was unwise enough to provide one), and stored them in her copious doctor's bag. Celery and radishes were added to the cache, as were leftovers from anyone's plate. That way, when she was on an urgent medical call, she always had something to eat. And, indeed, on a hectic day, last night's fixings were often all she ever did eat. She never had enough time, and meals were expendable.

This explains another of her unorthodox treatments, which left an entire funeral party convinced that radishes were an approved medical cure for depression.

The husband of one of her patients dropped dead of a heart attack at thirty-six. The patient took the shock very badly, and at the time of the funeral had not spoken a word for two days. The frantic family called Anna and asked her to accompany her patient to the burial, because they were afraid the young widow would break down completely. Anna arrived at the very last moment, bustled into the lead car, said a cheery hello to everyone, and settled down. She turned to the widow, gave her a long, shrewd look, then said, "Have you had anything to eat today?"

The widow said nothing, not even bothering to shake her head.

"Yes," said Anna, "that's what I thought. I've got something that will make you feel better right away."

Impressively she opened up her doctor's bag and fished around inside. One might have expected her to bring out a little white tranquilizer or a large full hypodermic.

Not at all.

Out of the professional-looking doctor's bag she prestidigitated a large dinner napkin, a Parker House roll, generously buttered, four radishes, and a saltcellar.

Hypnotized by the unexpectedness of it all, the young widow solemnly devoured the roll and the radishes. She looked around and said, "That was good." Then she started to cry her first real tears. From then on, she was all right. And she and the rest of the burial party were firmly persuaded of the magical properties of radishes.

As for Anna, she knew very well: "If you can't help them, feed them; it's all the same thing."

Mother and the Patients

FIRST AS A GYNECOLOGIST and obstetrician, and certainly as a marriage counselor, what Mother really practiced best was psychiatry of a particularly insidious nature. It kind of crept up on her patients.

For instance, as a gynecologist she was constantly being asked to perform abortions. Mother has always been an outspoken crusader for personal choice of any kind—including legalized abortion. But she herself will never perform even legal abortions. She sends them to another doctor. It is her belief that she became a doctor to save lives, not to take them. And she simply won't.

During the depression, when another mouth to feed often meant literal starvation for everyone, this was a particularly difficult decision for any physician. There was the woman who came to her hoping that the cessation of her periods meant an early menopause. (Of course at twenty-eight, it would have had to be awfully early.)

"Well," said Mother, "how wonderful! You're about two and a half months pregnant."

"Oh, no," said the woman I'll call Mrs. Smith, "I can't be. Doctor, you've got to do something for me, you just have to."

"Of course I will," said Mother, "but let's talk this over."

"There's no talking about it," said Mrs. Smith. "My husband hasn't worked for the last six months, and I'll lose my job if they even know I'm married. What would we live on if I did have the baby?"

"What does your husband do?" asked Mother.

"Well, he's willing to do anything, but he's a marvelous draftsman, and he's studying at night to be an architect."

"Wonderful," said Mother. "If he's such a good draftsman, I bet he'd be fine at lettering signs. I think I might be able to do something for him." She reached for the phone and called another patient.

"Hello, Mrs. Kettering," she said, "this is Dr. Daniels. Remember, you were complaining to me how hard it was to find someone to take care of your building? Well, I have just the man for you. And, listen, you told me how much that sign-painting company was charging you to put new numbers on the apartment doors . . . well, this man is a skilled sign painter, he'll do it for you for nothing. . . . Yes, yes, of course he can. . . . Why, he's a trained architect; he can do anything around an apartment house. Don't forget . . . you told me a four-room apartment went with that job. It has two bedrooms, doesn't it? No, of course he doesn't have a houseful of children, just a very beautiful wife. . . . Oh, you'll love them, I know you will . . . and they'll take wonderful care of your apartment house. Why, you'll be able to eat off your basement floors. . . . Not at all, you're very welcome."

"You see," said Mother, hanging up and smiling at a bemused Mrs. Smith, "now you have a beautiful two-bedroom apartment, your husband has a job, is there any reason in the world why you shouldn't have this baby? After all, how much can a little baby eat?"

"But I'm not sure my husband *wants* to be a superintendent. And you told that woman we have no children. What's she going to say when she finds out I'm pregnant?"

"Of course he'll be glad to do the work . . . it's really nothing, and he'll have all his evenings free to go to school. Why, he may even finish much earlier this way. It's perfect. You call him right now and tell him about it."

Mrs. Smith, dazed by Mother's enthusiasm and her own inconvenient condition, did, indeed, call her husband.

"Dan, listen—oh, I don't know how I can tell you," she wailed into the phone.

"Hello, Mr. Smith," said my mother, grabbing the phone away. "This is Dr. Daniels. I have wonderful news for you. I found you a marvelous job that gives you your own four-room apartment free. Oh, yes, you do need a four-room apartment; you're going to have a baby! Isn't that wonderful!"

She turned beaming to Mrs. Smith, "See, dear, he thinks it's all wonderful . . . the baby . . . the job . . . the apartment . . . and everything. You talk to him and see for yourself."

Mrs. Smith took the phone as though it had sharp teeth. "Yes, Dan. You *do* . . . you really do . . . you think we should have the baby? You want me to quit my job? But you'll be working as a superintendent. . . . Well, maybe you're right; maybe it would be good for you to have some experience with the practical problems of running a big building. You're sure about it?"

And the remaining months of her pregnancy Mrs. Smith passed in a happy daze of fixing up her nursery, lettering in apartment numbers (she was much better at it than her husband), and feeling nicely maternal.

This mood of the-best-of-all-possible worlds was somewhat dimmed when my mother delivered her of, not one, but two dimpled darlings. The nursery was really a little small for twins, but Mrs. Smith knew a *fait accompli* when she had one. However, her next visit to my mother was one of desperation. "Honestly, Doctor, I don't see how I can be pregnant again, but you'd better give me a test."

"No question about it," said my mother, "but it's great to

have your whole family close together. They'll be such good friends when they grow up."

"Well, of course, the twins are marvelous, but how could I possibly have another one? That bedroom is six feet wide. And Dan is only earning sixty dollars a month. And . . ."

"Listen, dear, you didn't think you could manage *one* before, and look how beautifully you are managing the two of them. Come on, what's so hard about having one more darling little baby? A year ago times were much worse. Your husband will get his degree before the new baby is born. You'll see; you'll laugh over this with me, this time next year."

I don't know how much laughing Mrs. Smith really did the next year. Once my mother delivered her triplets, she went and found another doctor.

At another time a very young, very newly wed girl came in, red-eyed and still weeping. She sat in the patient's chair at my mother's desk and told my mother that she knew she was pregnant; she'd tried everything she could think of, including horseback riding and rowing a boat all around the Central Park Lake. She just had to get rid of the baby.

Mother said: "Look, dear, I've got an office full of patients right now. I'll be glad to help you, but you just sit there and wait until I finish. Don't you worry about a thing. I'm going to take good care of you."

The young girl brightened perceptibly, feeling her troubles were all but over. She watched pregnant woman after pregnant woman go in. Each of them came out laughing at some cheery admonition of my mother's. Each of them seemed serenely happy at having achieved the miracle of creation. Finally, she was the only one left.

"Come on in," said my mother, "and let's talk about it. My, you're a pretty girl. You're going to have a beautiful baby."

"But you said you'd help me," sobbed the girl. "I can't have this baby." And she told the same depressing depression story

over again. Her husband had no job; they had barely enough
to eat; they had only just gotten married. To make it even
worse, her husband was in the theater, and even when everyone had a job, he often couldn't get work. Was this a world to
bring children into?

"Any world is a world to bring children into. Give them a
chance to make it better," said Mother. "Look at you. You've
got a whole marvelous life ahead of you. How can you be
afraid to live it? Listen, I know what you need, and it certainly
isn't an abortion. You need a pretty new hat! How long has it
been since you got yourself something extravagant, that you
had absolutely no reason to buy?"

"Not since we got married," said the girl thoughtfully.

"Well, do you want a new hat?" asked my mother.

"Honestly, Doctor, all I have is enough money to pay for
this visit, and it's all the cash we've got in the world."

"Oh, don't worry. I'll take care of you during your pregnancy and deliver the baby for nothing. Come on, let's go out
and get that new hat!"

And out the two of them went off on a hat-buying spree that
eventually resulted in a perfectly splendid baby.

Naturally, all her maternity patients did not come to her
wanting to be relieved of their condition. But a lot of them
were terribly anxious. They felt that no one else had ever had
a baby before . . . certainly no one else had ever had the same
kind of pains, or worries, or fears.

For the fearfully expectant she had one treatment, and it
always seemed to work. She would say: "Now everything is
perfectly normal. I just want you to do one thing."

"What's that," the patient would ask, immediately apprehensive.

"I want you to go out right now, sit down at a pleasant restaurant, and have a cup of coffee and a piece of very rich pastry
. . . the richer, the better. Then I want you to wait until five
exactly. At five o'clock I want you to be at Fifth Avenue and

Forty-second Street. And I want you to look at all those people going home from work. Then I want you to say one thing to yourself. Say, every single one of those people was born!"

Sometimes it wasn't apprehensive mothers but somewhat indignant fathers. There was the husband of the patient who was delivered of a nine-pound baby six months after she got married.

He came to see Mother very disturbed. "Listen, Doctor. I never touched her before we got married. Is it possible that this is my baby? It's awfully big to be premature."

Mother was in a quandary. She certainly couldn't betray a patient's secrets. Yet she didn't want to lie to a man who had come to her for an honest answer. She wasn't at a loss for long.

"Oh, well," she said, "this isn't too unusual. It only happens with first babies. You wait and see. I'm sure your next child will be full term." The man, seeing Mother's complete sincerity, was totally satisfied.

Mother Felt That Two Is a Necessity—and Nature Abhors a Single

As a child I never knew that maids ever came any shape but pregnant. Our maids were always girls who, through absolutely no fault of their own, had become pregnant. Their stories were always touching, hair-raising, and as divorced from the facts of life as possible. Either they had been sitting innocently in a movie theater when some nefarious stranger had given them an injection, and the next thing they knew they were in my mother's office getting a positive answer from that rabbit . . . or they had been walking along the street, minding their own business, when they were hit from behind, and the next thing they knew they were in my mother's office getting a positive answer from that rabbit . . . or, well, anyway, there doesn't seem to have been a conscious conception among any one of the girls "in trouble" my mother took in.

Naturally, since our maids were always pregnant there were a great many things they couldn't do. For instance, they never got up in the morning because they were always having morning sickness. My sister Thea, until she left for college, was in charge of breakfasts. Also, the girls couldn't do any heavy cleaning because, obviously, they couldn't be involved with anything heavy. What the three of us girls couldn't do was taken care of by a weekly handyman who, fortunately for the household, was a compulsive cleaner, and moved everything into the middle of the floor. On the other hand, he was so thorough that he often didn't have time to move everything back—so we sometimes went from week to week with a huge triangular china cabinet in the middle of the living room that was too big for anyone but him to move.

The nadir of our pregnant maids was one girl who simply couldn't stand the sight of food for the entire six months she spent with us. This meant Thea cooked two meals a day (lunch we ate at school), and Mimmi and I did the dishes. (After all, if the girl couldn't stand food cooking, she certainly couldn't stand it *after* it had been eaten.) As I remember, this maid left her bed only on Sunday mornings, to go to church.

However, Mother was never daunted by their interesting conditions. She happily provided these girls with room and board in return for nonexistent work, delivered their babies, and found good homes for them. If the girl could not be persuaded that adoption was the best thing for the child, she kept both girl and baby until the girl had found a good job. And she was determined to find them husbands as well.

She always believed every story told her about how a girl got pregnant; indeed, it was the firm conviction of Thea, Mimmi, and myself that, in spite of being an obstetrician, she still believed in the stork. She always knew the girls were from fine families. And above all she believed they would make wonderful wives. In my mother's house the only real wages of sin was having to go out with the men my mother found for you.

No tradesman could enter the house for any reason without being subjected to a long, exhaustive, and totally impertinent questionnaire about, first, his marital status, next—provided the answer to the first question was satisfactory and he was

single—his earning power, his prospects, his views on marriage and family, and, finally, on illegitimacy.

And, of course, no tradesman who was not single, with good
prospects and liberal in his outlook, could hope to keep my
mother's business. Since, even in the depths of the depression,
our grocery bills ran to $150 a week, and nobody ever checked
them or even added them up, the local grocers beat the bushes
to find personable, eligible, and liberal-minded clerks and delivery boys.

Our plumber would, unasked, deliver a panegyric on the
sanctity of motherhood and the hypocrisy of the marriage
vows. And our gardener was understandably bitter when he
was replaced, after he rendered himself ineligible by actually
marrying one of mother's rehabilitated maids.

The entire setup was slightly bizarre for three impression-
able girls, who got a somewhat slanted view on the prevalency
of white slavery, and eschewed all men because we knew for
sure if you mingled with men you became pregnant and had
to go to work as a maid.

Nevertheless, we somehow overcame the barriers that all
those stories had set up, and eventually we acquired beaus of
our own, much to Mother's delight. She was always cordial to
any of our young men, however exasperating or inappropriate
they were. When my sister Mimmi turned overnight at twelve
from a thumb-sucking infant into a full-blown Lolita, Mother
regarded her first caller with total equanimity.

"Hello," she said to the Filipino chauffeur who appeared at
our door carrying a huge and beribboned box of candy.
"You've come to call for Mimmi. Isn't that nice!"

"Yes, Madam," he said inscrutably.

"Well," said my mother, "how long have you known her?"

"We met today, on the beach. It is correct to call on her
here?" he replied.

"Oh, yes," said my mother cheerily, "of course it's correct.
She lives here."

"Good," he said. "I might see her?"

"Of course," said my mother. "Would you mind telling me how old you are?"

"I am twenty-seven," he replied. His English seemed to improve as he became more aware that there was something irregular in the whole situation.

"How nice," said my mother. "I'm so glad it doesn't bother you that Mimmi is only twelve."

"————," said the chauffeur in a long stream of Filipino, "but she told me she was nineteen."

"I thought she might have," said my mother.

"You will make her my excuses," said the chauffeur, clutching his candy tightly and trying to beat an instant retreat.

"Oh, wait a minute," said my mother. "You seem a very nice young man. Who do you work for?"

"Madam Strigler on Cayuga Avenue. This is my job only for the summer."

And with Mother's unerring eye for the polished diamond under the chauffeur's uniform, or the garage mechanic's coveralls, she discovered he was actually a medical student working his way through school and planning to go back and set up a cancer-research laboratory in Manila.

"Well, don't go away, please," said Mother. He was probably too good for our current maid, who besides being pregnant was somewhat simple-minded and probably *had* been hit on the head in a dark alley. But right next door there was a perfectly darling girl visiting who'd be delighted to go out with such a handsome and dedicated young man. One phone call, a swift direction to the chauffeur, an abrupt about-face, and he was off to a pleasant evening—which indeed turned out to be a pleasant lifetime together. It was love at first sight between the two—and, after all, my mother just happened to mention that the lovely girl next door was one of New York's most competent lab assistants!

I, too, had my share of undesirable or exasperating beaus. One was a boy with an absolutely incredible stammer. It was so bad that he frequently was unable to emit any sound at all, particularly on the telephone. And he invariably would call in the middle of office hours.

"Hello," my mother would say. "This is Dr. Daniels."

"   " said Michael.

"Hello, who is it?" Mother persisted.

"   " said Michael.

"Yes, what can I do for you?" she tried again.

"   " Michael replied.

"Oh, hello, Michael," my mother said, "I recognized you by your voice!"

On the other hand, if our beaus were occasionally undesirable, the beaus she would provide were even more so. Mother adored everybody. She rarely saw their faults. This might help her as a doctor, but it made her descriptions of men we were about to meet somewhat inaccurate.

"What's he like, Mother?"

"Oh, he's a darling!"

That phrase tended to overlook the fact that the man she was introducing you to tonight was a three-hundred-pound five-footer or an epileptic or cross-eyed or one-armed. On the other hand, a very high percentage of them *were* darlings. But you couldn't depend on it. Mother's judgment was not unqualifiedly accurate. In fact, she found it almost impossible to give up on a bachelor, a patient, or any human being. She saw everyone as basically good, no matter how much they tried to convince her otherwise. And on some occasions, she extended this benevolence throughout the animal kingdom as well. Once, when someone began vilifying a particularly vicious dog of Thea's who eventually had to be put away, she rose to the dog's defense. "What are you talking about? Freya is a lovely dog. So beautiful. By the way, has she stopped biting *little* children?" Therefore, one took her description of people with the whole saltcellar, not just a grain of salt.

All the same, on the two occasions when I really had to produce a man for a school dance, and for some reason was unable to, I appealed to her with equal parts of trepidation and desperation. Each of these times she produced a man so magnificent, desirable, and absolutely smashing that you could tell that she knew the difference between a darling and a dream.

She also had a succession of unmarried men who were for one reason or another not marriageable, even to her roseately glassed eye. These were known as Mother's bachelors. And, no matter how short, bald, unintelligible in speech, or long away from the loony bin—they were taken places hopefully by Mother.

Mother also had a large supply of young doctors, recent widowers, unexceptionable men. These were Mother's *shiddachs*. The *shiddachs* (a useful Jewish word meaning a prospective match) were often quite desirable. The bachelors never were. However, by virtue of the fact that if they were around long enough, Mother introduced them to every unmarried woman in New York, she eventually married off most of both categories.

Now, Mother needed bachelors. She was always squaring off triangles, taking out extra women, or winding up an extra woman herself and using them as escorts. When she finally married off the current bachelor, there would be much weeping, wailing, and gnashing—until another man hove on the horizon whom, obviously, no one would every marry.

A match dear to her heart, and one she'd been trying to effect for months, was for a lovely young divorcée who'd had a great deal of success as a permanent, floating understudy in Broadway musicals. She usually got to play the ingenue lead in the last two weeks of every long-run hit. If you get the idea she was a beautiful, delightful loser—you're right. And she had a positive genius for picking thorns in the garden of love. After her last romantic debacle, in which the man she had chosen went to jail for impairing the morals of a minor, and turned out to be a bigamist besides, this girl was understandably crushed. Mother had a long doctor-to-patient session with her, and told her sternly that she had to settle down with a solid citizen. Of course, Mother had already picked out the very solid citizen. He was a recently widowered judge who had been happily married for twenty-seven years, who was graying distinguishedly at the temples, who adored the theater, and who was—for one of my mother's matches—impeccably right.

Mother felt that nature must take a very perverse course indeed not to get these two together, and planned a theater party.

Since she was getting the tickets free, she also included her two most hopeless cases—her current bachelor, a rotund, balding man who liked to quote large passages from Marcus Aurelius in the original. At fifty-six, he had proposed to every girl he ever took out more than once without ever getting "yes" for an answer. Whatever he lacked was certainly essential. To this lack of appeal he added a distinct propensity for pinching any fanny that came within arm's length. An evening with him left you in a black-and-blue mood. His date for the evening was a determined "girl" in her fifties who had been married for two mad weeks she never stopped talking about and whose husband had departed after the honeymoon without a word but with their joint bank account. If she had been shy, she'd have been tolerable. But she was such an unmitigated extrovert that an evening with her demanded a rest cure.

Mother, having provided a pre-theater snack of sandwiches she had thrown together at the hospital (and if you've never had a cold-pork-chop-with-the-bone-in-on-bran-muffins sandwich, you don't know what eckk is), took them happily off to the theater.

Everyone had been so busy digesting her generous spread that they didn't get a chance to talk to each other before the first intermission. As they filed out of the theater, Mother's

bachelor began spouting Marcus Aurelius. "Oh," said the ingenue, "this is my favorite part." And to Mother's total cha-
grin she began quoting unintelligible ream after unintelligible ream.

"Gee," said Mother's bachelor, edging into fanny-reaching
distance, "you're the first girl I've ever known who even heard
of Marcus Aurelius."

"Well, of course he was really Antoninus," the ingenue replied. "I like him, but I really go for Epicurus. Do you know
this?" And another long stream of quotation came out, this
time in Greek instead of Latin.

Understandably, the rest of the group was finding it a little
hard to join in the conversation. At this point, Anna took
over.

"Dear," she said to the ingenue, "don't you want to tell the
judge about that marvelous part you have in summer stock?"

And she elbowed her way between the bachelor and the
bluestocking with great determination, all but turning the
poor girl head over heels in her effort to get her away from an
incipient fanny pinch.

"Yes, of course," said the ingenue, "I'm doing a whole season of summer stock: Laurie in *Oklahoma,* Julie in *Carousel,*
and I'm even getting to play Laura in *The Glass Menagerie*—
that's a part I've always wanted to do." The judge mentioned
courteously that he could see why, he had seen Julie Haydon
in the original version, and she had a true Julie Haydon quality.

That was the last word the judge said to her all evening. It
was time to get back to their seats. They all laughed happily at
the comedy. Then came the second intermission.

As they were going up the aisle, Mother's bachelor finally
got within pinching distance. The ingenue turned a glowing
smile on him, and lowered her lashes. "You know what Epicurus says about the pleasure principal?"

Since this was the most encouraging reaction he had ever

gotten, he was only too happy to hear. And the two talked Latin and Greek for the rest of the intermission.

Meanwhile, the bachelor girl began to take heart. She turned to the judge, and said, "I loved that production of *The Glass Menagerie,* too. But I hardly noticed anyone but Laurette Taylor."

"Most people didn't," the judge said, and began a lengthy discussion of "unappreciated performances I have seen."

After the first two, the bachelor girl was smart enough to wait until he mentioned the maid in the first act or the brother in the third before she began distributing encomiums. Anna watched what was happening in noisy despair, injecting a frantic "Come over here," or, "Why don't you two join the fun?" all to no avail. By the end of the second intermission, the two couples had cheerfully redistributed themselves— the ingenue and the bachelor exploring pleasure principles side by side, the bachelor girl and the judge agreeing that the young girl third from the left at the end was giving the best crowd-scene performance they'd ever seen.

For the first time, it occurred to Mother that her bachelor girl bore a very strong resemblance to the judge's first wife. She took a good look—yes, a very strong resemblance. Well, *beshert* was *beshert,* and fate was fate. And she went home happily, having made two matches and lost a bachelor.

"Now, you see," said Mother when she got home to us, "you're always telling me I shouldn't try and marry people off. There are four miserable people who are going to live happily ever after." Mother's career as a marriage counselor had never dimmed her optimism.

"But," we pointed out, "no one in their right minds would ever have planned either of those matches. Not even you!"

"I don't know what you're talking about," said Mother, sublimely happy; "it all turned out exactly the way I wanted it."

And not even the two eventual divorces would convince her otherwise.

Summer Was Always
A-Cumin In

ALTHOUGH THE FAMILY finances fluctuated almost as alarmingly as Mother and Daddy's marital barometer, poor or rich, the family summered together. Poor, it meant that as many as twenty-six of us (sisters, cousins, aunts, permanent boarders, etc.) would be crammed into a four-room bungalow. Rich, it meant that two or three adjoining houses were taken over and turned into a kind of Chinese family enclave, with meals taken together, evenings spent together, beach populated together, but sleeping done separately.

At the center of the enclave was, until she died in 1937, Elka —known to her grandchilren as Baba. Israel had died in 1922, leaving a clear field to the benevolent matriarchy of Elka and her three girls. Both Harry, Mary's husband, and my father regarded the matriarchy with complacent eyes as a rather pleasant feminine stronghold. So the women were free to band together. Whatever the finances and the servant situation, there was Baba, cooking marvelous Jewish delicacies with which she regaled us and the many guests. Unfortunately, however much she cooked, the sea air and our ravenous appetites guaranteed that there would not be enough.

The one exile (and that's the way she was regarded by the rest of the family) from the summer enclave was Sophie, who married my Uncle Jack and promptly proceeded to go to places like Point Lookout and Massachusetts for the summer. When they finally bought a house in Bayville at the other side of Long Island, far away from the family's beloved beach, we all retaliated by buying property only a hillside away, accumulating two houses there and moving Mohammed to the mountain. Ours was a difficult family to escape from.

Perhaps my Uncle Jack's reluctance to join the enclave at Atlantic Beach was explained by his first introduction to it. Although he had courted Sophie for a number of years, including the time she was engaged to someone else, he was really exposed to the family in all its glory only a short time before the wedding.

He had then been invited out to the house for a weekend, in the semiofficial capacity of an about-to-become groom.

It was a relatively affluent year. Mary and Harry and their two children were living in their own home, but, as always, we all ate and beached together, from the Danielses' home at Nassau Avenue. This had an upstairs porch where I spent my entire summer, sunning, playing, reading, and practicing hanging by my heels from the porch banister. It was my mother's conviction that one day I would fall off.

Jack had just arrived and been put into a room to change, when my sister Thea, down at the beach, was ducked under water for too long by a playful friend. She went into laryngeal spasm, and almost drowned. My two cousins, Ernest and Bettina, were carrying her home amid a great deal of hullabaloo. A neighborhood dog ran out and bit my cousin Bettina sixteen times on the leg. Mary, watching her firstborn bleed copiously all over the pavement, ran toward the house, yelling for my mother and screaming *"Das kind, das kind, Annele; das kind, das kind."* My mother heard her screaming, and since the only *kind,* or child, she thought to be disaster-prone was I, she immediately decided that I had, as she had feared for so long, finally fallen from the balcony and brained myself. Unfortunately, when she made this decision she was in the shower, for she ran out stark naked into the street to pick up the pieces.

Not unnaturally, the considerable hubbub had accumulated quite a crowd, who were interestedly watching Thea in spasm and Bettina dripping blood. They became absolutely fascinated by the spectacle of mother in the raw.

Sophie desperately tried to console both frantic mothers, and succeeded in getting air into Thea so she stopped gasping for breath. Bettina eventually stopped bleeding, although she still bears the scars of every one of those bites. As Sophie was shepherding the last person into the house, a new thought occurred to her as she saw her intended dazedly watch the entire procession march into the living room.

"Poor Jack," she said, "poor, poor Jack."

It speaks well for my uncle that he married into the family anyway. And it certainly explains the house in Bayville.

All those summers somehow telescope into one golden time in my mind. We were all together. There were long days after long days spent in the sun. Except for the defection to Bayville, which took us to a muddy-bottomed creek to swim and which lasted mainly through the war years when the Atlantic Beach houses rented for phenomenal sums, we spent every summer on the beach. Mary, Anna, and Sophie produced seven children (one doctor apiece), but wherever we traveled we all came back to summer.

Eventually, Anna's girls grew up and got married. Thea and I eloped, thereby cheating the family of a spectacle. But Mimmi, always Mother's good girl, had a real wedding. It was to be a small family wedding, but as one invited guest said to my mother, "Anna, how could you possibly have a *small* family wedding?"

With typical insouciance and disregard for climate or season, my mother planned an outdoor wedding in Atlantic Beach for September 23. The week before the wedding was a ghastly one. Foggy, damp, cold, and unfestive. Mother showed no inclination to shift the site. She had done her duty. She called the caterers and told them to prepare something suitable for a few people. Surreptitiously, Thea and I started the current maid (who was fortunately Italian and a great cook) making mounds of edibles for the hordes we knew would descend.

Mother then called the rabbi. The conversation, which was taking place in the dining room while we were all eating breakfast, went something like this. She was pleased to be making arrangements for the wedding march. "Rabbi," she said happily, "when I spoke to you before, you mentioned that you had a portable organ. Can you bring it to the wedding?"

At this point someone started to giggle, and all was lost. My mother threw us an agonized glance.

"Oh," she said into the phone "it's your *wife* who plays the organ. . . ." How that conversation finished, no one at the breakfast table ever found out. Mother must have kept enough of her equanimity to get the rabbi, his wife, and his organ to the wedding, however. They were all there.

The night before the wedding, Mimmi having been put comfortably to bed, Mother, Thea, and I were talking over the arrangements. Providing the weather cooperated, the wedding was to be in the garden, which was in full fall bloom.

"All those chairs on the lawn will face the *hoopah*," said Mother. The *hoopah*, in Jewish weddings, is a canopy that is held by the witnesses over the heads of the bridal couple. Thea and I looked at each other. There had been no plans made for a *hoopah*; it was twelve o'clock at night; and however portable the rabbi's organ might be, we couldn't start asking him at that hour to bring his own canopy.

It was useless appealing to Mother. She felt that the Lord would provide the weather, and undoubtedly the *hoopah*, as well. Thea and I snuck out into the dark. Atlantic Beach is well supplied with boardwalk. We meandered casually down to the beach and came to a boardwalk ramp that was made in sections. Quietly, we lifted up the ramp. It came loose quite easily. As surreptitiously as possible we carried the six-foot length of boardwalk ramp home. That would do admirably for a platform. Then we spent the rest of the night stapling hydrangeas onto a length of purple velvet. That was the *hoopah.* And supported by two broomsticks and two mop handles, it served brilliantly the next day, when, with the Lord acquiescing to my mother's optimism, the sun shone brightly. The weather produced a record high, but Thea and I trembled throughout the ceremony that the two policemen directing traffic would recognize the missing section of boardwalk under the bridal couple's feet, and arrest us all.

Mother Was Always Having Babies

As a busy obstetrician, Anna was frequently called away from gala evenings to deliver a baby, and almost every birthday party I ever had was punctuated by my mother walking in and saying, "Happy Birthday, it's a boy!"

She startled many a cabdriver by hailing him in full evening regalia and saying: "Hospital, Maternity entrance, and hurry!" While she was young and skinny, these rides may have been harried but they weren't harrowing. But as she got older and a little more rotund, they often rivaled Paul Revere, as the driver dashed through traffic yelling, "The baby is coming, the baby is coming!"

Usually, she was able to correct this impression quickly, but on one snowy night she gave her usual direction to a driver who had a particularly thick glass partition between the driver's seat and the passengers. The ground was very slippery, and after one startled looked at Mother the cabdriver started skidding all over the cobblestones. He took off in third gear, gunned his motor and gave the gas all he had. After all, he knew an emergency when he drove one.

Anna rapped aggrievedly on the glass. "Slow down!" she shouted. "I've got time."

The cabdriver heard the rapping but nothing else. He stepped on the gas even harder.

"Slow down!" shouted my mother, rapping furiously.

The cabdriver skidded through a red light and turned the wrong way down a one-way street. My mother took off her shoe and started rapping with it on the glass. "Stop, I tell you! You're going to kill us both. That baby will wait. It's a primip."

Even if the cabdriver could have heard her, he wouldn't have recognized medical slang for a first baby. It is a conviction, unsupported by fact, among many obstetricians that a first baby takes days to be born.

Anna saw it was hopeless. She assumed the suggested crash position on airplanes, head between her knees, hands clasped behind her neck, and waited for the worst.

When the cabdriver finally got her to the maternity hospital, he leaped out, opened the door, and gazed flabbergasted at Anna's bent body.

"Did you have the baby, lady?" he gasped, as he watched her unfold.

"Of course not," she snapped. "The baby's in the hospital. And young man, if you go on driving that way, you'll be there, too." And she swept through the revolving door, leaving behind her a very perplexed (and, incidentally, unpaid) cabdriver.

Another time, when she was driving in her Whippet, this time to deliver the seventh baby of a mother who had once delivered on a subway train because she thought she had plenty of time to get to the hospital, she was breaking all speed limits.

Behind her she heard the rise and fall of a police siren, but she simply had no time to stop. However, the policeman on his motorcycle soon caught up to her and stopped her with the customary question about a conflagration.

"Oh, Officer," said Anna. "I can't stop to get a ticket now. I've got to get to the hospital; I'm going to deliver a baby."

The policeman took one look at her undeniably rounded figure, and stepped off the running board.

"Come on lady," he said. "I'll get you there. God bless you and God speed!"

And for the first time in her life, Anna's rapid progress through the red lights of Queens had official sanction.

When they got to the hospital, Anna jumped out of the car, threw the keys to the cop, and said: "Here, you park it. I haven't got time."

It was a somewhat nonplussed policeman who, having stopped for a well-deserved beer in a local pub to drink the health of the unborn baby, came out an hour later just in time to see Anna getting back into her car.

"Are you all right, lady?" he asked. "What was it, a false alarm?"

"Oh, no," my mother said cheerfully. "A beautiful little girl. Thank you so much."

"But, lady," expostulated the cop, "you can't leave now."

"I have to. They're waiting for me at The New York Infirmary." And off she drove, as he watched it without believing it.

The Green Uncle and Bezbal

WITH THE GREAT UNREST in Europe, a whole new wave of immigrants began coming over, once again to escape war and a new, organized, and massively efficient pogrom that was to be dignified by the name of genocide. Our share in it was *"Der Greener"*—which was translated for us children as "the green uncle." For months and months we heard about the green uncle who would be coming over to stay with us. We were all very excited. We were assured we would love him, and we were perfectly prepared to. Much to Anna's consternation, when we were allowed to go to the pier to meet him, we all behaved terribly. As he walked down the gangplank and embraced Anna and Maurice enthusiastically, we all burst into tears.

"But, children," said Anna, totally nonplussed, "this is your green uncle you've been waiting to see."

"He isn't green at all," said my sister Thea accusingly; "he's exactly the same color we are!"

Once we'd resigned ourselves to the fact that we didn't really have any Martian relations, he turned out to be quite nice, if unreasonably hipped on the subject of bezbal, which was all he'd talk to us about. He had enthusiastically studied up on American manners and mores, knew a great deal more about batting averages than we did, and seemed somewhat disturbed not to walk off the boat into Lou gehrig's arms. He was considerably mollified a few minutes later when he elicited from us the information that we went to the same school as Babe Ruth's adopted daughter. He settled back in great satisfaction; obviously America was going to be everything he'd dreamed of; his family was already consorting with royalty!

Names none of us had ever heard of—we were not a sports-oriented family, and there were no young boys to quote us batting averages—fell from his lips with great ease and in peculiar accents. Anna was quite at a loss.

Finally she broke in on this totally incomprehensible monologue to tell the green uncle about his new apartment, and discuss with him what he might want to do by way of work. The possibilities were limited by the businesses available in the family. At twenty-six he was unlikely to go into doctoring. Tailoring attracted him not at all. Real estate was, to a European Jew, simply incomprehensible. How could you make money buying and selling land and houses when, if people were lucky enough to have a tiny piece of land or a house, they hung on to it for the life not only of themselves but of their entire family? After no more than ten minutes of animated discussion, he decided on insurance. This, too, was an incomprehensible profession—you were betting people that they wouldn't die—but apparently in America that was a bet you could win.

The future having been disposed of, the green uncle turned to my parents and asked when it would be possible to see a real game of bezbal.

"Is there a game today? Could we possibly go now?"

"But," said my mother, for once in her life nonplussed, "don't you want to see the rest of the family? And you have to take your things to your new home. And see that, too. Of course, if you really want to go to a game today"—she was beginning to catch his enthusiasm: what better introduction could there be to America than a baseball game?—"I'll see what I can do."

As always, when it came to getting tickets for anything, Mother Knew Someone.

She left us with the green uncle, ice-cream sodas, and baggage while she went to call a friend who had a box at the Yankee Stadium. One of the few names she had recognized in my uncle's long discussion was Babe Ruth, and he played with the Yankees. Her friend said Yes, there was a game today, and, No, he wasn't using his box, and certainly she could use it. Since it was only eleven o'clock in the morning, there was plenty of time at least to get rid of the baggage, and say hello to a few relatives.

When these preliminaries were taken care of satisfactorily, Anna left us off, fobbed off the relations with a story about taking the green uncle to see about a great job, and they were on their way. Though the green uncle had no basis of comparison, the seats were truly superb, right behind the first-base line. Mother got into the spirit of the thing by buying absolutely everything that was being hawked, so that before the game began the green uncle, who had already had an ice-cream soda and a liberal helping of my grandmother's cooking, was loaded down with a hot dog, popcorn, peanuts, beer, and a Yankee banner to wave, if he could find a hand to wave it with.

He was tremendously excited: his favorite fantasy about America had come true, and he watched all the preliminary warm-ups with great enthusiasm, managing to nudge Anna and point out such extraordinary things on a baseball field as a man throwing a ball and another catching it. Anna was perfectly willing to be impressed. She knew absolutely nothing about baseball, and had never seen a game before.

At last the cry of "Batter up!" filled the air. It was enough of the drama; now the game was actually going to begin! My uncle was beside himself with delight.

The first pitch was delivered. The batter hit a high foul that made a right angle along the first-base line. A very right angle. Suddenly my uncle's first baseball game was over. He had been beaned!

He was carried out of the ball park, totally unconscious, to a waiting ambulance, and spent the next two weeks in America recovering from a bad concussion. My mother's explanation was: "How did I know that baseball is a very dangerous game? People are always sending little children to ball games!" After that, she confined her treats to new arrivals to the theater and concerts. Few people have ever been beaned by a violin bow.

Entertaining Mother— and Vice Versa

ENTERTAINING MY MOTHER held many hazards. Aside from her propensity for arriving four hours late for any occasion, she took the *politesse* of "My house is your house" quite literally.

If you were so rash as to invite her for even the most intimate occasion, she would show up with an indeterminate number of people. To all of them she had extended with great warmth and sincerity your personal invitation. "Mrs. Nixon particularly asked me to bring you!" is the way she would react to a White House invitation, and she'd react that way to everyone she met along the way.

Since she saw nothing out of the way about serving a dinner cooked for two to ten or more, she never understood the violent distress of a hostess with six perfectly prepared Rock Cornish game hens who was suddenly confronted with four unexpected guests.

"Just cut up my portion," she'd say, "or scramble a few eggs. After all, they don't care *what* they eat!" In Anna's house, at least, this was perfectly true. If they cared, they knew enough to eat before they came.

Yet Mother managed to group around her those who were

most eminent and/or notorious—social lions and pariahs
who formed a nucleus of *"tout* New York" and who could certainly have gotten a better meal for the evening almost anywhere else.

If she was coming to you, she was sure to arrive with one or
more marriageable daughters in tow. (I often think that the
kindest thing my family ever did for New York society was to
marry both my sisters off very young and to ship me off to
Paris.) This, as much as any other aspect of Mother's be-
haviour, distressed hostesses who carefully balanced their
tables and their sexes. They took to inviting her at the last
minute, hoping that way to keep her from having time to invite
very many other people. But at least one memorable cocktail
party this technique backfired spectacularly.

True, Mother, having gotten an invitation for five thirty at
five, was hard pressed to bring anyone along. But she decided
to go by subway, and while shuttling through Grand Central
Station she happened upon six Russian sailors. This was during World War II, when Russians were persona grata in even
the most capitalistic congregations, and Mother began talking
enthusiastically to them in the best Russian they'd heard since
they'd left Vladivostok. Since the sailors spoke nothing else,
they fell on Mother like a long-lost mother. However, there
may have been a slight communications gap nonetheless.
"Come with me to meet some marvelous people," she said.

"Girls?" asked the sailors eagerly.

"Girls!" said my mother happily. *"Da, da!"*

"Da, da!" said the sailors.

My mother, an enthusiastic matchmaker, envisioned a virtually unlimited new vista opening up for her, with all those
American girls settling down with the Russian Navy.

The sailors may have had a somewhat less permanent arrangement in mind. In any case, they followed my mother
very happily, convinced they had hit a new high in American
hospitality.

They took their introduction into an extremely posh and impeccably aristocratic Park Avenue duplex with good grace. Though the girls were in décolleté, they were also robed in unmistakable respectability. One hopes the sailors didn't instantly assume that every American lived exactly like this millionaire manufacturer of noodles, coffee, and soap—but they were worldly-wise enough to see that it wasn't the kind of house they'd been hoping for.

Making the best of a good deal, they downed vodka-spiked champagne, ate huge amounts of caviar—assuring Mother, fortunately in Russian, that it was a most inferior kind—went wild over deviled eggs, which they'd never had before, and proceeded to become the life of the party.

They kasatskied, orchichorniaed, oy yuchnaed, and da-daed to the regalement of all. They set up a Red Navy chorus that consisted of the cream of American capitalists. And finally, they went tunefully off, ensemble, seeking a more instantly available brand of girl.

For weeks afterward, that poor hostess was besieged with requests from her friends for "that marvelous troupe of Russian dancers," and her best friend stopped talking to her for a full year when she couldn't produce them.

For months, into the next social season, Mother was invited to the city's most elegant gatherings, with the totally unnecessary proviso that she bring anyone she liked. A succession of bewildered hostesses greeted a motley crew of daughters, patients Mother hadn't had time to treat in the office, and casual pickups—none of whom was Russian, dressed for the occasion or who, alas, proved to be the life of any party.

But if you ran a risk entertaining my mother, that was nothing to the risk you ran being entertained by her. A scarcity of food at dinner was the least of it. Her really sinister invitations were reserved for those she asked out to her beach house, on a hot day, to go for a swim.

Poor Bill Liebling, who was at that time one of Broadway's most sought-after bachelors and a great actor's agent, unwisely accepted an invitation on a terribly hot Saturday to go out to the beach for the weekend.

"Listen, Billy," she said, "we'll get into the car, drive out to the beach, and have a marvelous swim. Don't think about it. Just say Yes!"

Billy, who knew my mother very well and should certainly have known better, said, "Yes!"

"Okay, I'll pick you up in twenty minutes; all you need is your bathing suit."

Two hours later she did arrive in a raddled old taxi that looked as though, not moths, but piranhas had been at it, plus a driver. The driver was perched unaccountably high on his seat, and the back seat was more than filled with three large adults, plus my mother, who was, of course, very small. Billy was not a large man, but he did require an inch or so of seat. There wasn't one. Both the front of the taxi and most of the floor in the back were entirely taken up with huge cans of paint marked "Navy surplus—battleship gray." The driver was perched on a paint drum; there were at least four huge large cans in the back; and the people already in the car had somehow disposed of their legs around, about, and on top of them. One of the ladies—unfortunately the fattest of them— cheerfully got out.

"I'll make the most room if I sit on someone's lap," she said good-naturedly, and there was nary a lap in sight but Billy's. Ever the gallant, he tipped his hat and murmured what a pleasure it would be; but, undeniably, the lady would make him two or three lapfuls.

"There," said Mother in obvious satisfaction, "now we're all nicely settled. Is everybody in? I'll just slam this door." And they were off.

But off to where? The cab went a little way, maybe twenty blocks, and stopped. Billy, who could not see out from under

his behemoth, assumed it was for a particularly long red light.
That was until my mother stepped out of the cab.

"I'll only be a moment," she said, "I promised just to look in
on this patient for a second before I went away for the weekend. I'll be right down. Does anyone want to go to the bathroom? Don't be shy and get a honeymoon bladder!" For the
first time, Billy was aware that they had stopped outside a large
hospital, and stopped right underneath a large sign that said
Hospital Zone: Positively No Standing at Any Time. Of
course, the minute Mother left, a policeman arrived out of nowhere. The cabdriver blanched and said, "Quick, does anyone
here have a license? I knew I shouldn't have left mine at home,
but the doctor wouldn't let me go back for it even for a minute. She said she was in a hurry."

Billy said he had his license. "Listen," said the driver,
"when I get out, you get out too, and we'll change places, see.
You make like you've been driving all along." Squeezing,
grunting, and managing all the same to be unobtrusive, Billy
got out from under and over to the driver's side of the cab.
The two men were standing looking unconcerned when the
policeman hove down on them.

"Which of you is driving this—ah—thing?" he demanded.

"I am," said Billy bravely.

"You can't read, huh?"

"Certainly I can read, Officer, but I was carrying a doctor
on an emergency call, and she insisted I let her out here. She'll
be out any minute, and she'll explain it herself."

"Emergency, huh?" snorted the policeman. "I suppose all
the rest of these people are doctors, too, and you run an emergency ferry. And I suppose all those cans of paint are for a
dying battleship—a paint transfusion, huh? Listen, buddy,
I'll say this for you: you got guts! Gimme your license. Okay,
now where's the registration?"

Billy looked frantically at the driver, but apparently the

registration was kept permanently in the glove compartment, and that at least was all right.

"Okay, buddy, see you in court. Emergency, huh!" The cop finished writing out the ticket, and for the first time Billy realized that it was not an ordinary parking ticket but a personal traffic violation that would require his presence in court.

"Here," he said, passing it on to the driver. "This is for you."

"No, it ain't. It's your name is written right down here." Billy bowed to the inevitable.

By this time considerably more than a minute or even a half hour had passed, and there was still no sign of Mother. The passengers in the back were beginning to get a little restive, and one of the ladies said, "Say, what is a honeymoon bladder? Maybe I'd better go inside, after all." The exodus toward the hospital waiting room left only Billy and the driver waiting outside.

The other passengers returned and settled themselves; that is, they got into the car, sat for about a minute in the blazing interior, then got out again and held a council of war. They seem to have come to some conclusion, but never disclosed what it was, because at that moment Mother appeared. Her usual exuberant cry rang out, *"Mazeltov,* it's a boy!"

Only Billy was churlish enough to complain, mostly to himself, about the fact that she had kept them all waiting for almost two hours. The others were delighted to be in at a birth.

Finally, the trip got under way again. This time they must have covered at least ten of the twenty miles of their journey before the car stopped. Billy, whose vision was again totally obscured by the large lady on his lap, confidently expected to see sand dunes and ocean. No such thing. When his burden got out to stretch her legs, he discovered they had never left home.

"Where are we?" he asked anguishedly.

"In Brooklyn. It's right on our way, and I'm just stopping

off to talk to my painter," said Mother. She was building a bungalow in the country, which explained both the painter and the paint.

She came out a little while later, looking really distressed. Since Billy had seen her go through flood and fire without so much as drooping her smile, he began to be alarmed. Only a major national catastrophe could have caused the Anna Daniels he knew to look so upset.

"What's wrong, Anna?" he asked fearfully.

"Could I talk to you a minute, Billy?"

He hastened out of earshot of the rest of them, and waited for the worst.

"Bill, the painter absolutely refuses to come out unless I pay him in advance, and I don't have more than six dollars on me. How much do you have?"

Unfortunately, Billy was in the habit of carrying a great deal of cash with him. "Well, Anna, how much do you need?"

"Do you have three hundred?"

"Yes, but do you need all of it?"

"Well, he won't come unless I pay him."

Resignedly, Billy forked out three hundred dollars. Then it occurred to him that the painter was probably also going to ride in the car. He ran after Mother to get back his money. No investment of his was going to put one more person on his lap.

He arrived in time to see the painter and what must have been his son loading themselves and their equipment into a truck. "Okay, Doctor, we'll see you at the beach," said the painter. Billy was so relieved that he didn't have the presence of mind to beg a ride in the comparatively empty truck.

"Come on Billy," said my mother, "don't you want a swim?"

Since by that time Billy had been en route for about three hours, he very much wanted a swim.

Miraculously, with many stops and starts but no further detours, they did indeed arrive at the beach.

"Here's the bungalow," said Mother.

Billy waited until the weight got off him, and then he descended, considerably flattened. Thin to begin with, he now looked exactly as though some mysterious process had dehydrated him, and he would have to be reconstituted with the addition of water. Moreover a cold wind was blowing. Mother always said the beach was twenty degrees cooler than the city, but never before had this been brought home to him so forcibly. He looked at his watch. Well, no wonder. It was already five o'clock!

"Come on," said my mother, "let's hurry and get a swim while the sun's still out."

The rest of the people in the car emerged, felt the ocean breezes, and demurred.

"Come on, Billy. You're a real he-man. Let's go for a swim and leave the sissies here."

Thus appealed to, what could a man do? Billy changed hurriedly into his bathing suit and gooseflesh, grabbed a sweater, and for the first time noticed the size of the bungalow Mother had invited him to. It consisted of two rooms, a hall, and a kitchen. It occurred to him that Anna had her whole family (us) out there. We must be at the beach. There must be someone watching us. He mentally added up the number and sexes of the people in the car. It was an awful lot of people, none of whom seemed suited to a mass orgy.

"Say, Anna," he asked, "where is everyone going to sleep?"

"Oh, don't worry," Mother replied, "I have the whole bungalow next door, the one I'm building."

Billy's fears were assuaged; after all, a whole bungalow must have some sleeping accommodations. He started for the beach.

"See," said my mother, pointing to a half-finished structure that did have walls and spaces for windows and even the framework for the roof, "there's plenty of room there for everybody!"

Billy slapped a few mosquitoes, looked at the windowless windows, and said thoughtfully, "I see." He walked pensively down to the beach with her, stood at the water's edge while she swam in the icy froth, impervious to a gale that was blowing up from the north.

"Anna," called Billy, "you'd better come in; it's raining!"

"Oh, I'm wet already," she assured him blithely, and swam on.

By the time she got out, he was fully as soaked as she was.

"Just a minute," she called, "I want to get out of this wet bathing suit."

Fortunately, there was no one else on the beach braving the inclement weather, because Billy would never have survived Anna's idea of a modest change out of a wet bathing suit. This consisted of putting on an unfastened bathrobe, stepping out of her suit, stepping into another one, and then, and then only, fastening the robe. From the back it was a circumspect performance; from the front it was instant nudism.

They walked back to the house, the rain having let up to a determined drizzle.

Billy took another look at his roofless abode for the night.

"I've got lots of blankets," said Mother.

Billy wondered if they were made of rubber.

They came into the bungalow, where they were instantly greeted with hot soup. It was delicious, and did much to cheer Billy up, until he realized that it was probably all the lunch and supper he would get.

"Say, Anna," he said, "where can I pick up a pack of cigarettes around here?"

"There's John's; it's only four blocks away. It's a bar and restaurant, but I'm sure he must have cigarettes." At those magic words "bar" and "restaurant," Billy's ears stood right up and wiggled. "I'll be right back," he said. Off he went, carefully avoiding taking any of his fellow guests. They looked happy and perfectly satisfied. While he had gone for a swim, they'd probably had a six-course dinner. He hightailed it over to John's.

Over a double whiskey and a mammoth hamburger he considered his situation. He seemed destined to spend the night with a group of strangers, sleeping on the floor of a roofless bungalow. He hadn't had a swim. He was likely to freeze to death during the night, and he was out three hundred dollars, which, if he knew Anna, was not going to be instantly repaid. Billy did the only possible thing. He called his secretary at home. "Listen, do me a big favor. Send me an urgent telegram to Anna Daniels' house in Atlantic Beach saying I have to be in the city tonight."

The telegram arrived. Billy made his apologies and took the cab off to the train station. In the warmth of a speeding train he relaxed happily. He was about to have a wonderful time, a good sleep, in a warm bed, in the city!

About one thing he was absolutely wrong. Mother started paying him back the three hundred immediately. She came in the next week and gave him shots against cholera, diphtheria, bubonic plague, and Rocky Mountain spotted fever.

"If only I were going to India, Anna," he murmured.

The next week she started him on a series of Vitamin B-1 and liver shots.

"These will really build you up," she assured him.

"I don't know if I can stand being built up any more. Anna. Those shots hurt."

"Well, they're good for you. They're the latest thing. Everybody's getting them—Toscanini, Stokowski, Paderewski—"

"But, Anna, those people are all fifty years older than I am, and doing strenuous work. All I do all day is sit. I don't need to be built up."

Her answer to this was to appear the next week with two mammoth bottles, one of aspirin and one of vitamins.

For the next ten years she appeared regularly with shots, vitamins, wonder drugs, antibiotics, antihistamines. Most of them were huge cartons of samples. And as Billy said: "I'm ashamed to stay so healthy. But since Anna's given me every shot known to man, how can she expect me to get sick?" He never did get three hundred dollars' worth sick, but, as he put it, "I must have had at least two thousand worth of preventive medicine already."

The roofless bungalow Billy only just escaped calling home had its own place in Mother's life, and a rather feckless place it was, too. Originally, she had planned to build it the year before. But, as frequently happened, money was so tight that plans had to be postponed.

She had wanted something very modest, to match our current finances, a two-room plus-kitchen bungalow that would be centered on one narrow lot. It was too bad that the property was so narrow, but Mother could afford only one plot. This meant it was virtually on top of the adjacent bungalow, owned, fortunately, by friends, and frequently rented from them for the summer.

When Mother acquired enough money to go on with the building, she looked over the plans happily. It was exactly what she wanted.

"But Mr. Dancer," she said to the architect, "where is my porch?"

"What porch, Doctor?" asked Mr. Dancer.

"Well," said Anna, "you can't have a bungalow without a sun porch. I want it in the back of the house so I can sunbathe all I like without having people stare at me."

If Mr. Dancer didn't know why people should stare at my mother sunbathing, it was only because he didn't know her propensity for stark nakedness. Our neighbors certainly did.

"Well, Doctor, to add the supports for an upstairs sun porch, I'd have to widen the building slightly, and that would be a violation," ventured Mr. Dancer.

"Wonderful. That means the whole house will have more room, doesn't it? I think it's a little skimpy now, don't you?"

Since Mr. Dancer had labored long and hard to produce a

bungalow that contained all Mother's requirements in two rooms and a kitchen, he did not think it was skimpy, but he murmured something under his breath that she could take for polite acquiescence. He went home to widen the bungalow and add an upstairs sun porch.

"Well, now, that's exactly what I wanted, Mr. Dancer; but as long as you have the sun porch taking up all that space, couldn't you have an enclosed porch . . . like a sleeping porch underneath? After all, it will have a roof and everything already. And won't that be nice? We'll have an extra room!"

This time what Mr. Dancer murmured under his breath could not be taken for polite acquiescence by anybody. "Doctor, how are you going to get to the sleeping porch? The only way is through the bathroom, and you can't have people traipsing through your bathroom."

"Why not?" asked my Mother reasonably, leaving Mr. Dancer totally silenced. "Well, anyway, you have to build a stair up to the sun porch, and if you just put a door under the stair, people can go in and out without coming into the house at all. It will be like a separate room, and I can rent it out if I want to." If Mr. Dancer lost his aplomb as he imagined where the rest of us would be sleeping if my mother rented space in a two-room plus-kitchen beach house, he said nothing but, "Yes, Doctor."

But he had opened up whole new vistas for Mother. If she used the bathroom as a kind of hall, she could put in another bedroom after the bathroom and before the sleeping porch. Of course, that, too, would be a kind of hall, but it would unquestionably double her sleeping space.

When Mr. Dancer came back with his revised plans, she was full of her newest recommendation. He listened without saying a word. The next day he came back with a plan that did indeed have a real hall, very narrow, but a hall, off which there were three bedrooms leading into the sun porch.

"Now, that's exactly what I wanted!" said Mother delightedly, "but why are we wasting all that space on a hall? I wonder if . . ."

"Doctor," said Mr. Dancer firmly, "we are wasting all that space on a hall because someone, sometime might hear that I designed this house—a gross canard I would appreciate your not repeating—and I cannot allow you to construct a railroad flat in the middle of a stylish beach resort. You cannot add another room to these plans because you are right now building six feet farther out than you are allowed to, and you will have a violation that requires a variance. You are also two feet wider than you are allowed to be, which requires another variance. These are my final plans. Here."

"Well, I told you it's exactly what I wanted. Don't worry about the variances. I'll take care of it all."

Contrary to what one might expect, no one complained, and the variances were unnecessary. The next-door neighbors seemed delighted to have us living in their living-room windows. And while they were somewhat startled to find a building modeled on their square small house take on the proportions of a pregnant dachshund, they were by no means distressed.

The problem arose from quite another source. Anna got an overdue tax bill for the lot on which she'd built the bungalow. "That's funny," she said. "I know I paid that bill, and I'm sure that's not the right lot number. They've made a mistake." The next bill she got said that the lot would be sold at auction unless she came down and paid it. Fulminating against red tape and the stupidities of local officials, she gathered up all her papers and went down to prove that she had paid her taxes on the lot. And of course she had—on the lot she had bought, two lots down from the one she built on.

Quick reconnaissance uncovered the fact that the bungalow had actually been built on a lot owned by a Mrs. Simons of 1042 Park Avenue, New York. Mother, nothing daunted, put in a telephone call to her.

"Mrs. Simons," my mother said into the phone briskly, "about that lot on Second Street, Lot Number 192, I might be interested in buying it if the price is right."

"Oh, yes," said Mrs. Simons, "you mean those two lots next to the Rickmans. I certainly want to sell."

"But I want only lot Number 192." Money was still very tight.

"Well, I'll tell you; I'll go out and look them over again. If it looks to me like I can build on one lot, maybe I'll sell you the other."

All Mrs. Simons had to do was to go and look over her lots! It would be too much to expect her not to notice that there was a house on one of them. "No, no, don't bother," Mother said quickly. "What's your price for the two of them? . . . My goodness, *that's* out of the question!" And never one to admit that she was in no position to bargain, Mother managed somehow to cut the price in half. The transfer was made in record time, since Mother had to buy the lot before Mrs. Simons happened to see it.

But the day after the closing, Mrs. Simons did stop by.

"How in heaven's name did you get that house up so fast?" she demanded.

"Oh, you know," said Mother, "it's all prefabricated."

Still, people couldn't help asking, until she sold the bungalow, why, with such a huge amount of land around it, she built a long, skinny house right on top of her neighbors.

Mother and Mickey the Plumber

MOTHER WAS AS GENEROUS with everyone else's services as she was with her own. She was likely to volunteer people for the most unlikely tasks, and always endowed them with skills of which they were totally innocent.

Mother rented one of her beach houses every year to a tenant who returned with the unrelentingness of the locust. Why, was a mystery, since Mrs. Humpelmyer liked nothing about the house, and said so quite often during a summer. Mrs. Humpelmyer apparently *did* eat off her floors, and her arrival was always announced by an infinitesimally grimy forefinger pointed accusingly.

"I ran my finger over the floor, and look how dirty it got!" That was her hello.

"But, Mrs. Humpelmyer," my mother would say righteously, "I've had a couple out there for four days cleaning the house. They're Germans. They are very good cleaners."

"Humph," said Mrs. Humpelmyer, managing with that one sound to impugn my mother's veracity, the nationality and morality of the couple, and the cleanliness of the house.

On the other hand, my aunt, who also rented out her beach

house, had less dependable but far more amiable tenants. This year's group were three young cloak-and-suiters who had made it big by mass-producing one of Balenciaga's most popular coats in four days. They had stolen the design, cut, sewed, and sold it in record time, and were now reaping the substantial rewards of this legal piracy on the high fashions.

They were young men with impeccable clothes, but somewhat peccable New York accents, who were awed to find themselves in Atlantic Beach and were scared to death of my aunt. They wouldn't have dared to complain that there was anything wrong with their cottage's appointments, although the front door, in fact, could neither be opened nor closed.

My mother remembered that my aunt had not been out to the cottage since last fall. She determined to pay a visit to see if my Aunt Mary's tenants had gas, light, and water—niceties my aunt was quite capable of overlooking. As she was walking out the door on this errand of mercy, the phone rang.

"Dr. Daniels," the rasping voice of Mrs. Humpelmyer complained, "my kitchen sink is stopped up, and I have ten people coming for dinner."

"All right, Mrs. Humpelmyer," said my mother, "I'll do what I can."

At 5:00 P.M. on Saturday, Mother knew her best would be absolutely nothing. Plumbers at the beach in the first week in July did not answer emergency calls unless they came between ten and twelve on a weekday.

Mother set off for Aunt Mary's cottage, wishing she were the one who had three young and undemanding tenants.

"How is everything?" she called jovially to a young man on the lawn, happily drinking in the sun and a gin and tonic. "I'm Dr. Daniels. My sister is your landlord. Is the electricity turned on?"

"Oh, yes," said the young man, "it's lovely, lovely . . . only . . ." His hesitation was obvious.

"Yes?" said my mother encouragingly.

"The front door won't close. Is there some trick to working it?"

"Oh, no," said Anna, "it *never* closes."

Her tone carried great conviction, and the implication that closing one's door was a form of depravity.

"Of course," said the young man conciliatingly, "of course."

"What's your name?" asked my mother, a new thought occurring to her.

"Mickey Fetter, Doctor," he replied.

"Well, Mickey, do you know anything about plumbing?"

"Oh, I try to make myself useful around the house . . ."

"Marvelous!" said my mother. "Can you fix a stopped-up kitchen sink?"

"Do you have tools?" asked Mickey dubiously.

"Yes, yes, everything," my mother reassured him.

"Well, I can try," said Mickey, casting an anxious eye at his white silk shirt and brand-new white flannels. "I'll get a jacket."

This proved to be a magnificently tailored captain's blazer in flawless navy-blue flannel. Again he regarded his clothes anxiously. Not to the most complacent eye could they have been called the Right Thing for going plumbing.

"Let's take my car, Doctor," he said. Sitting behind the wheel of his brand-new Cadillac convertible reassured him. "Now, where are the tools?"

"Just stop off at my house," she said. "I've got everything you'll need."

She directed him to her house, and as she came out again it dawned on him that it wasn't *her* kitchen sink he was fixing. He was nonplussed, but felt too committed to back out now.

"You're sure you got what I need, Doctor—a plunger, a wren—"

"Everything you need," said Anna confidently, indicating a paper bag under her feet in which she'd placed her plumber's tools. "Now turn right."

They arrived at 332 Nassau Avenue before Mickey had a chance to ask any more questions.

"Mrs. Humpelmyer," my mother called out joyously, "I was so lucky. I found a plumber."

Mrs. Humpelmyer appeared.

"This is Mickey, Mickey the Plumber."

Mickey climbed sheepishly out of his car. His social sense was uncertain at best, and an introduction like this might well have floored Amy Vanderbilt. Blindly he headed himself toward what he hoped was the kitchen.

"That's right, Mickey," said my mother. "Right through there."

Mickey recoiled in horror from a truly loathsome sink, filled with scummy water, potato peelings, and other unrecognizable debris.

He took off his perfect blazer and hung it carefully over a chair. He rolled up each of his silken sleeves deliberately. "Doctor, where's the tools?"

Handing over the paper bag, she looked at him sternly and said, "S-h-h-h."

The admonition was necessary. The bag contained a hammer and a box of carpet tacks.

"Do your best," said my mother encouragingly. Then she sidetracked Mrs. Humpelmyer efficiently.

"Now, Mrs. Humpelmyer, show just where you found that pile of dirt you phoned me about yesterday."

Some of it must have been under the kichen sink, because when Mickey emerged his white flannels were tattletale black and his shirt was a Chinese hand-laundry emergency case— but, miraculously, with Anna's plumber's tools, he had unclogged the sink.

He was putting on his blazer again when Mother and Mrs. Humpelmyer returned. "All fixed," he said happily, not unreasonably expecting some praise from the woman.

"Look at that mess," said Mrs. Humpelmyer.

"While the handyman is here," boomed my mother overridingly, "is there anything else you want him to do?"

Mickey knew the handwriting on the wall when he heard it. He took off his blazer and, in a very good imitation of the TV plumber who sells Duz, said, "Lead me to it." He thereupon performed some tasks, including repairing the roof, for which a hammer and tacks were more appropriate tools.

He was helped in his labors by Mrs. Humpelmyer's young Swedish maid, a girl whose rear action he had been admiring since he walked in. Blue-eyed, blond-haired, and a sexpot in any language, she held the hammer and tacks in a fashion so appealing it should have been illegal. Having finished his labors, he once again put on his blazer and led my mother back to his Cadillac.

"Goodbye, Mrs. Humpelmyer," my mother said, "wasn't it lucky I found a plumber?"

At the corner Ingrid, the maid, flagged them down—her blond hair and perfect bosom glowing in the sun.

"Say," she said, "I seen many plumbers, but in America the plumbers they been kings. My night out is Thursday."

"Okay, Thursday," said Mickey, obviously delighted.

He double-clutched the Cadillac off with a mighty roar.

"You know, Mickey," said my mother, "she's from a fine family in Sweden. She's working here *au pair* to learn the language."

"Yeah?" said Mickey, enchanted at the prospect of all that bosom and culture too.

"Yes," said my mother. "Now, just drop me off here. And thank you so much. You're a lovely boy. I'm sure your mother is proud of you."

"Well, thanks, Doctor. Thanks a lot. You think it's okay for me to go out with her?"

"Surely. You young people enjoy yourselves."

"Thank you." And, as all my mother's greatest impositions always seemed to do, it ended up with Mickey thanking her profusely for the opportunity of being her plumber, handy-man, chauffeur.

The next day when Mrs. Humpelmyer called to complain about the upstairs toilet, my mother snapped, "Be reasonable, Mrs. Humpelmyer. I *had* the plumber there yesterday!"

Mother vs. the Empty Bed

PERHAPS BECAUSE of her early experiences in this country, when she felt that she had a mission to house and feed the unlucky, Mother abhorred a vacuum even more than Nature does, if it involved a bed. Let there be an unoccupied bed in any of her houses, she fills it.

When her circumstances became affluent, Mother began collecting houses and beds with total abandon. It was unsafe to drive her past a "for sale" sign. With her, houses were like peanuts; she couldn't be trusted to gobble down just one. Fortunately, she liked to sell her houses almost as much as she liked to buy them—otherwise, we might be the land-poorest family in the world. She did once own four houses in Atlantic Beach and two in Bayville at the same time—but for the most part her holdings were in a state of flux, and only she was certain which she possessed at any one time. Sometimes not even she was.

For instance, she sold a house in Atlantic Beach and then really forgot she had done so. When some friends came in from the coast, she blithely offered them the house as a temporary home until they could get settled. They went off happily with the keys and proceeded to install themselves very comfortably. Knowing my mother well, they were somewhat amazed at the stylish—yea, even *decorated*—mood of the furnishings. Most of Mother's homes were Salvation Army Shabby in style. This one was determinedly French Provincial, with a number of quite valuable pieces. "Well," said Mr. Coleman, "Anna must really be coming up in the world."

"Oh, you know Anna," Mrs. Coleman replied. "She bought the house furnished, and hasn't really been down to take a good look at what's in it." With housewifely fervor, Mrs. Coleman put dust sheets on the best pieces, confined her children to an upstairs playroom, and proceeded to clean up everything as a thank you to my mother.

This was terribly lucky, because two days before the Colemans were going to leave they were awakened by a loud banging and an official, "Open up!" in the unmistakable tones of the police. Somewhat startled, they did indeed open up to find themselves facing the irate owners and the local constabulary. "What are you doing in our house?" asked the real lady of the house, echoing the indignation of Mama Bear.

"Why, this isn't your house. Anna Daniels loaned it to us until we could find an apartment. We've been here for three weeks. Ask anyone!"

"I don't have to ask anyone. I know you have. That's why we came back from Florida, because a neighbor wrote us to say what a nice couple we had hired to take care of the house, and we knew we hadn't hired anyone at all." By this time the lady of the house had had a chance to glance around. "Why, you *have* taken marvelous care of it, haven't you? And how did you ever get the spots off the rug? I've tried and tried, and never could!"

The policeman, seeing that this dramatic confrontation was deteriorating into helpful hints for the housewife, murmured that everything seemed to be under control, and could he leave now? Everyone cheerfully sped him on his way; the owners and borrowers settled down together over the owners' twelve-year-old Scotch, and the lady of the house said she wouldn't hear of the family leaving before their apartment was ready.

"I suppose I'd better call Dr. Daniels and remind her that we bought this house," she said, "or God knows who she'll send to be caretakers next."

The lady of the house really got off lucky. In her own home Mother filled the beds with people who were inclined to take the bed with them when they left, as well as anything else that could be moved and didn't breathe. Fortunately, the only possessions Mother really cared anything about were the houses, and those couldn't be stolen. To say that Mother's impromptu boarders were light-fingered is grossly to understate the case. They were more like light-bodied, and would walk out absolutely bulging with the things we might have considered family heirlooms, had they ever stayed long enough in the family to be inherited. In fact, Mother's boarders made a great mistake to steal anything. There was more Japanese about her than her eyes. You had only to admire anything—it didn't really matter what—and she happily handed it to you. This rather openhanded attitude also pertained to any of *our* possessions. It wasn't good in my family to treasure anything. It was bound to disappear. And if you remonstrated, Mother would say, with every appearance of incredulity: "Was that something you *wanted?* Why, if I'd known that, I'd never have given it away."

Mother came by this attitude naturally. Elka came to stay with her for a few weeks in the winters. She usually lived with my Aunt Mary, who didn't have a maid, and therefore allowed her to clean, cook, and baby-sit to Elka's heart's content. When her other daughters begged her to come for a visit, or to live, her answer was always the same: "I love you, darling, but what would I *do* in your home? You come to me, I'll cook you a little something." Elka found a great many things to do. Among the things she found to do was to straighten and clean out drawers, a job that could not properly be left to any maid.

My father, Maurice, was at that period going through a Beau Brummel stage, and he had just gotten six custom-tailored Sulka shirts, which—even in those days—had cost a small fortune (or, in fact, not so small a fortune). He was very proud of them, and they reposed in splendor with a drawer to themselves, while his more plebeian shirts were crammed into another one. Elka opened up the shirt-jammed drawer. The depression was still on, and Elka, of course, was still as public-spirited as she had been in her cold-water flat days. *"Tcha, tcha*—so many shirts for just one man, and so many men without any. It's wrong. It is a shameful thing; I must do something about it."

She counted out seven shirts, one for each day. Then she counted out another three; after all, a man had to have his clothes washed, and a very fastidious man might want to change his shirt more than once a day. The rest of the shirts she threw on the bed. Then she opened the next drawer— more shirts! The Sulka shirts joined the others on the bed. Off went my grandmother to Hadassah. And some surprised shopper in a thrift shop was the lucky recipient of five un-worn silk Sulka shirts. One hopes the custom-tailoring fit.

When my father came home, he was too agonized even to be angry. He just quietly went to his closets and took all his Savile Row suits out for a cleaning, being careful not to pick them up until after Elka had left. But whenever she came, the first thing she did was head for my father's bureau to see if he had more than ten shirts in it. Needless to say, if she was ex-pected he never had, and at no time were his custom-made shirts left out where she could find them.

Mother's extreme hospitality meant that we often had very interesting guests. The titled daughter-in-law of a world-famous writer, herself a convert to Zen forty years before any-one else had ever heard of it, came for dinner and stayed two years. That was when I first moved in with the diathermy machine in Mother's office. The guest "borrowed" my room.

We also had the nineteen-year-old scion of a very wealthy family, his girlfriend, who was ten years older than he, and their newborn baby. Mother put them up in a maid's room in which she could never have asked a maid to sleep. We all understood that this was a temporary expedient until he could persuade his family that they ought to be married. Unfortunately, his family proved obdurate, and the three of them seemed likely to become permanent adjuncts. Finally, my mother reluctantly felt called upon to point out to them that the room was really too small for one person, let alone three.

"I'm awfully glad you pointed that out, Doctor," said the young man. "And now that the Countess" (that was her title) "is leaving, we thought you'd put us in her room."

I've rarely seen my mother annoyed by any imposition made upon her. However, even she seemed to feel that this was a little too much. "I'm sorry," she said. "I need that room for my daughter."

"But," said the young man, showing he had perfectly absorbed the to-each-according-to-his-needs spirit of the house, "there's only one of her and *three* of us!"

Mother held her ground, or my room, and that was one of the few instances in which our nonpaying guests left unwillingly, grumbling loudly that they were being dispossessed.

Another facet of Mother's extreme hospitality was that she ran a sanctuary for erring husbands. Men who had left their wives and had nowhere to turn were likely to show up for a night or a week. Sometimes we'd see them with young women, who we were always told *were* their wives. After Mother had managed a real reconciliation, something she was remarkably good at (because after two or three nights in our house any man had to appreciate an ordinary household and a normal wife), Mother would gather us all together.

"Now listen, girls," she'd say, "when Mr. Jones comes in tonight to see us, he'll be bringing his wife with him. Don't mention he was ever here with anyone else." John's Other Wife was pure fact to us!

The traffic in our house became so confusing that one night an overnight visitor got totally lost and wound up in my mother's bedroom. My father, fortunately, was away.

"Mimmi?" said the guest hopefully. Mimmi's was certainly the most attractive bedroom he could have blundered into. She was back in residence because her husband was in the army.

"No," said my mother, waking from a sound sleep totally calm and sitting up in bed. "Mimmi's room is three doors to the right." And with that she lay back down again and went soundly back to sleep. She seemed to have no curiosity whatever as to who was asking for directions to her daughter's bed.

In fact, it was not unusual to find disconsolate people simply looking for empty floor space where they could put down a rubber beach mattress they'd been given to sleep on. I guess Mother really started the whole concept of the hippy pad.

There was one occasional resident who posed a unique problem. He was Captain Mac. He was sincerely devoted to my mother, and often chauffeured her around and did odd jobs. He was also a periodic drunk. During his drinking bouts he swung from Jekyl to Hyde. Drunk he was his normal self, pleasant, devoted, and well behaved if you ignored a decided list to starboard. Sober, he went on a rampage of destruction.

So when he started drinking, Mother had me follow a specific routine. I would go to bed early and be awakened at about six. Then I'd get up and lock myself in the bathroom. I'd stay firmly locked in while furniture and dishes flew and I heard my mother's cheery voice saying, "Now, Captain Mac, why should you want to do that?" As the sounds of mayhem lessened and the D.T.'s waned, I'd wait for Mother's knock. When she had him fully calmed down, she would come and tell me to let myself out. The moral I drew from this has stayed with me all my life: Beware of drunks sobering up!

Yet no matter how murderous Captain Mac's attacks were on furniture and innocent bystanders, he never once raised even his voice to my mother.

Captain Mac also made himself useful by taking care of whichever houses Mother owned at the time. His background was extraordinary. He really had at one time been a sea captain, and had even spent time in the Arctic on one of the polar expeditions.

When some other stranded friends of Mother's came into town in midwinter of 1947, she sent Captain Mac out to Atlantic Beach to unfreeze a totally unheated house, put in as many electric heaters as were necessary, and get it into shape to receive the family. Hardly had the young couple settled themselves in and reactivated an old furnace that hadn't been used in years, when they got the news that the husband's father had died and they would have to leave for the funeral in Detroit.

The wife called Mother and told her she was leaving but that everying would be all right; the children were in the hands of the family's maid, and if anything was wanted, her brother in New York would take care of it.

The day after they left, the Blizzard of '47 began. The frantic parents couldn't call, didn't get any answers to telegrams, had visions of a frozen house, starving children, and a totally abandoned family.

It took them three days to get transportation home. When they arrived, they had to dig their way through the streets to their house with a shovel. They walked into a warm, welcoming home, filled with laughing babies and a calm, cool, and collected maid.

"How have you managed? What happened? Where did all this food come from?"

"Oh," said the maid, "Dr. Daniels comes through with a sled and snowshoes every morning. She brings milk and wood and even the paper. She should be here any minute now."

And a few minutes later, Mother and Captain Mac, who had improvised a dogless dogsled and snowshoes, came into the house.

"Welcome home," said Mother. "I hope you weren't worried. After all, you knew I wouldn't let your babies stay out here alone."

"But there hasn't been any traffic out here for three days. It took us a whole day to get out. How in heaven's name did you make it?"

"Well," said Mother, "when I heard it was the worst blizzard in fifty years, I sent the captain out to find a jeep, and we just started driving. After all, in this weather, none of my patients will make it to the office."

"Anna, where did he find a jeep in the middle of a blizzard?"

"Listen, dear, if I asked him questions like that, he'd tell me. And why should I have to worry about the answer? He found one; it got us out here. For all I know, he owns a garage full of jeeps."

Mother's impromptu delivery service was so efficient that for years it became part of the town's snow-emergency program.

Marriage Counselor, Heal Thyself

MOTHER AND DADDY'S MARRIAGE could not, in its last years, be called a marriage at all. It was a series of confrontations, separations, desperate regroupings, and attempts at holding on to an irreversibly deteriorating relationship. They tried. Noisily, lovingly, antagonistically they tried. And then Anna, finally, realized there was no way out.

Among the couples for whom she served as a marriage counselor was one about whom she said privately, "The only solution to their problems is divorce." However, she worked valiantly to keep them together, secretly sighing with relief when the couple finally stopped seeing her.

Her own opinion was that the husband in this case was a man any woman would be lucky to get. But, of course, she maintained a therapist's impartiality. After they were no longer patients, circumstances threw Anna and the husband together. They met coincidentally at friends' homes. They seemed often to turn up at the same places at the same time. They began joking about it.

The husband, who in due time became an ex-husband, was Richard. He was a quiet man, but even in an extremely volatile family like ours he had only to utter a word to end discussion, argument, or pleading. He was a small man, with a shock of prematurely white hair and beautiful blue eyes that could twinkle or squelch with equal effect. He had a mordant wit that took the form of laconic and definitive comment.

And he could not have been more different from my mother had you been deliberately creating negative and positive poles. Their courtship started slowly and casually. He was charmed by all that was so different about my mother —her total disregard for any of the conventions, her appearance of complete scatterbrainedness that concealed an ability to juggle family and demanding career without apparently letting either suffer.

She found in him what she had never been able to find with my father—a warm, secure relationship that enveloped and protected her. In place of challenge, there was reassurance; in place of great valleys and highest peaks, a steady, everyday affection that was always there, as were the loving arms and steady hand that shielded her from life instead of challenging her to conquer it.

"Richard is here," Anna used to say with a great, upturning lilt to her voice. No one who heard her say it once could believe that those three words meant anything to her less than "God's in his heaven, all's right with the world."

After Richard got a divorce in Reno, Mother took the final step of breaking with my father. And on April 30, 1941, a Florida Supreme Court judge pronounced Richard and Anna man and wife. From then on, everyone seemed determined to unpronounce them.

Now that these two had found each other, and their romantic troubles were ended, their other troubles seemed just about to begin. Richard's first wife, understandably upset at losing a husband where she had expected to get him back—at her marriage counselor's—took her grievances to the courts and the newspapers.

The courts (in a decision that took up a column in the august *New York Times*) decided that they weren't legally married in New York. Florida said they were legally married in Florida, and since that's where they were married what was the fuss?

The frantic lawyers threw up their hands and suggested that Mother and Richard move to California—or New Jersey. Both of them agreed that, since they had demanding professions that kept them working till all hours in the city, in the city they would stay. After all, they spent three months or so a year in Florida where they were *certainly* legally married. Wasn't it kind of fun to live in sin in New York?

Then the newspapers took over. They had a lot of fun with headlines like "Statistician Goes for Cute Number" and "War of the West End Wives." The three of us children, who were inclined to think of my mother, Anna, as a back number and this marriage as a December-December romance, were understandably startled to read that one tabloid felt that roly-poly, frankly grandmotherish Mother was the "svelte, redheaded thirtyish Dr. Daniels."

Since Anna had never cared for public opinion, Richard was learning that with Anna around he had better forget it, too. The three of us girls—one married, one engaged, and one only just turning nubile—took the attitude that this was one of the funniest tempests ever stormed up in a teacup. We all moved into a huge apartment on West End Avenue and started discovering how to be one happy family. For the first time, we all had a resident father figure who took his paternal duties very seriously. Since Mother's response to any problems we had was to act as though they weren't there (and surprisingly often this treatment did make them disappear) it was a novel experience to have someone around who was interested in your troubles, listened to them, and then *did* something about them.

Whether it was getting into the college of your choice, getting out to where your husband was leaving for overseas military duty, or not getting that call from the one boy you'd be caught dead with at the senior prom, Richard would listen, make a suggestion or two, and then quietly go about making this the best of all possible worlds for his stepdaughters to live in. If he couldn't make a beau call, he could remind you of another one who would do. If he couldn't keep a new husband from being sent overseas, he could provide a home and loving attention to a left-behind bride. And if he couldn't get you into the college of your choice, he had a friend who was Director of Admissions at a better one.

Somehow, for everyone in the family there came to be one solution to every problem that faced us. All of us began to say in Mother's lilting tones, "Richard is here." And until his death in 1962, those three words meant that, no matter what, everything was going to be all right.

Mother and the Three-Minute Egg

RICHARD WAS an extremely precise man. Very successful as an insurance actuary—a profession that required the utmost attention to detail—he had, until he married my mother, lived a careful and well-arranged life. He was rarely late by a minute for an appointment. He expected his meals to be served on time, piping hot, and perfectly prepared.

Nothing in his life had ever prepared him for living with Anna. Her maids, if not pregnant, were generally so incompetent that no one else would hire them, or so old that they couldn't get around anywhere else to apply for a job. In spite of the fact that she paid excellent wages and made few demands, she always seemed to wind up with the lame, the halt, and, in one case, literally the blind.

When we occasionally pointed out, and Richard forcibly insisted, that the present incumbent was really impossible, Mother's answer was always: "But how can I fire her? She's seventy-eight. Where else will she get a job?"

At the time Anna married Richard, our maid was an ex-Follies girl who was delighted to raise her skirts over her ample thighs and demonstrate the number she'd done in the chorus but who was absolutely incapable of getting dinner on the table before ten o'clock at night.

Richard put up with this ultrafashionable dinner hour for a while, and then pointed out that their cocktail hour was so long he arrived at the table absolutely sloshed, a situation he found neither seemly nor desirable.

Mother said reasonably: "But even if Minnie did feed us earlier, I'd still have to see my patients. You know a lot of them have to come in in the evening. I explained all that to you before we got married."

"Anne, dear," said Richard, "evening is from five till seven thirty; after that it's night. And I will agree to no arrangement that keeps your nights from being mine."

It was such a nice honeymoon thing to say that Mother actually rearranged her office hours, even if she couldn't do very much about Minnie's dinner hour. However, she did start having Tip-Toe Inn send up a hundred hot hors d'oeuvres every night, and that assuaged Richard's hunger until Minnie very fortunately left. The only bad result of that contretemps was the ten pounds the lengthy hors d'oeuvres hour put on around his middle.

Since the next maid to come along put them both on a strict version of the Duke University rice diet, the extra pounds were soon taken care of. After that, Richard used to interview the maids before they got in to see Anna, and life became somewhat more conventional, although he never did succeed in establishing a fixed dinner hour.

More serious to his actuarial mind was the fact that Anna could never arrive anywhere on time. After years and years of obstetrics, she couldn't adjust to the idea that her present marriage-counseling practice did not involve hospital emergencies. She was so used to arriving for dinner after the after-dinner cordials, and saying, "Well, I just stopped off to deliver a baby!" that it seemed much too tame to arrive at the appointed hour.

The first time Richard walked in with Mother and discovered he was four hours late for dinner, he started murmuring the marriage vows to himself: "For better and for worse." The second time, he simply put his coat back on and went home. And before the third time could occur, he took matters into his own hands.

As soon as Anna mentioned that they were going out somewhere, so he wouldn't make other plans for the evening, he phoned the hostess. "Please call Anne and tell her that three of your guests have to make a plane and that dinner is being served at five thirty," he said.

The hostess laughed. "Oh, we're used to her; we really don't mind at all; we just keep a hot plate."

"Well, I do mind," said Richard. "Please call her."

"All right, I'll be glad to," said the hostess, "but for God's sake don't show up before eight."

In fact, they came in about nine, in time for a very quick predinner cocktail, but still in time for dinner. Mother had such a good time eating with everyone else that she didn't seem to notice that no one had left to catch a plane.

The next time they were invited out, Anna, who really was trying to please Richard, told him she'd meet him there, and promised to be on time. When he arrived at the right time, his hostess' greeting was somewhat strained. "Anna's been here since a quarter to five," she said. "She wanted to surprise you!" After that, if Richard pushed the hour ahead, he was careful to bring Mother with him.

There was one situation between them, though, in which only love triumphed. That was in the making and serving of a three-minute egg. When Anna married Richard, he explained to her that one thing he was really finicky about was a three-minute egg. He expected one every morning, and he expected it to be right, and above all, he expected his wife to prepare it for him.

Anna was perfectly willing. She always was up to have

breakfast with Richard. In fact, she was usually up much earlier, attending to her voluminous correspondence. When Richard said, "Good morning, dear," she went in, kissed him, continued through to the kitchen, got an egg, took it in with her to the office, put it to boil in the sterilizer, wrote three or four more letters, took out the egg with a surgical clamp, and went back into the kitchen to get the eggcup and bring it to the table.

The first morning she did this, Richard tasted the egg, smiled fondly at his bride, and said "Nice try, Anne, but not quite right."

And, indeed, the next morning he got up ten minutes early, went and got Anna to come into the kitchen, filled a pot with water, waited for it to boil, put the egg in carefully, turned the timer upside down, watched the sand run out, ladled the egg out and placed it in the eggcup, and turned to Mother and said, "There, Anne, there's a perfect three-minute egg."

The next morning—and so it was every next morning of their happily married life—Mother went in and kissed Richard "Good morning," kissed me in passing, continued through to the kitchen, got an egg, took it in with her to the office along with the three-minute timer, put it to boil in cold water in the sterilizer, wrote three or four more letters, absentmindedly turned the timer over three or four times as well, took the egg out with a surgical clamp, laid it down on her desk while she stamped the letters, and went back in the kitchen to get the eggcup and bring it to the table.

Richard tasted the egg, smiled fondly at his bride and blew her a little kiss, and then turned to me and said, "You see, I taught Anne how to make a three-minute egg!"

In fact, neither of them really changed. Richard remained prompt and precise; Anna remained precisely as ever. And yet they both seemed to get places at the same time. As Anna was fond of saying about her most unlikely matches: "You never know till you try. And then you can always try a little harder."

Mother and the Presidents

ON TWO SEPARATE and memorable occasions Anna came into contact with Presidents of the United States. In both cases they were recent ex-Presidents. In both cases she made quite an impression herself.

The first time was while she was still an undergraduate at Cornell. Teddy Roosevelt was making his Bull Moose campaign to regain the Presidency. He was visiting the campus to win votes and influence people. But of course he was welcomed, not as a candidate but as a President. The president of Cornell gave a special tea for him, to which were invited selected students. These students were allowed to pass cookies and lemonade, make themselves useful, and be introduced as a special honor.

Among the honored students was Anna Kleegman. Roosevelt was particularly interested in the achievements of the recent immigrants to the United States. He did all he could to further those achievements, and Cornell felt that there were very few of their students who achieved quite as much in as little time as had this young girl from Borschevka.

When her time came to be introduced and her credits had been given him, Anna flashed a brilliant smile at Roosevelt, looking way up at him. Her tininess was particularly apparent next to his huge bulk.

"Well, Anna Kleegman," he said in his booming voice, "do you know that you owe me your life?"

"I'm grateful for it, President Roosevelt," she replied, "but how did you save my life? I think this is the first time we've ever met. I know I could not have forgotten it if I'd ever seen you before."

"You never saw me, little girl, but I really did save your life," said the President. "When did you come to the United States?"

"In 1906, Mr. President," said my mother.

"And do you remember that just before you came, there was supposed to be a big pogrom in your area, probably right in your town?"

"Yes, because that is one reason we left. But the pogrom never happened. We were warned and we were waiting, but it never happened."

"No, and I'm the reason that it never happened," said the President. "Just when the pogroms near Kiev were planned, I was acting as peacemaker in the Russo-Japanese War. You'll pardon my saying, my dear, that the Russians had lost the war. I was trying to get them the best possible peace terms."

"Yes," said my mother, fascinated that so august a person had ever heard of Borschevka and the pogroms, amazed to know how this powerful American President could have had any effect on her own fate or even bothered himself with it.

"Well, I simply will not have religious persecution or killing in the name of Christianity. I told your Czar that if he didn't put an end to these terrible pogroms of his, I wouldn't arbitrate the peace for him. And I meant it, too; he could see that I meant it, and he listened to me. So you see, little girl, if it weren't for me, you might very well have been killed in a pogrom. And even if you hadn't been killed, you would probably not have come to America."

"Oh, President Roosevelt," said my mother, "what a wonderful man you are! And I want to make you very glad that you saved the Jews of Borschevka. I hope that for my life, which you saved, I can save many, many, many American lives. I am going to be a doctor. And, you'll see, I'll be a good doctor. How hard I will work for America and for you!"

Roosevelt, obviously moved, patted her on the shoulder, and then turned to the other guests and began talking to them. But before he left, he went looking for her again to say goodbye.

"Remember, little girl, you have a big job to do, and I do believe you are going to do it. Keep hold of that ambition, and if you do, nothing can keep you down."

There was a long time between Roosevelt and Anna's next President, Harry Truman. Anna had gained a great deal of self-assurance in between. And certainly no man looking at her would ever again call her "little girl," because she had also gained quite a bit of weight.

President Truman had just completed his term in office and just married off his daughter to Clifton Daniel. He and Mrs. Truman were taking an unofficial trip to Europe, and happened to be staying at the same hotel in Rome where my mother and Richard were.

She was attending a medical convention, and walked into the dining room wearing her delegate's badge, which had her name in large letters, ANNA K. DANIELS, M.D.

As she walked in, her eyes lighted on the President and Mrs. Truman quietly eating their breakfast at a secluded table. Mother had long been an admirer of the President's, and after all she had married off three daughters and innumerable other people's daughters as well. She felt a great affinity for Truman, one that he was, of course, totally unaware of. With her jaunty, bobbing walk, she bustled over to Truman's table full of smiles and goodwill.

"President Truman," she laughed exuberantly, "President Truman, I want to wish you *mazeltov* for Margaret!"

Truman looked up quickly. The Jewish word had caught his attention. It was one even he knew. "Thank you," he said very pleasantly, laughing with my mother.

"You see," continued Mother, pointing to her name tag, "she married into the *mespucha*. I'm a Daniels, too!"

She and Truman then proceeded to have a pleasant conversation that was interrupted when Richard came over to remind her that she had to be at the meeting because she was supposed to give a paper in fifteen minutes.

Actually, Mother was very good at using Jewish for effect. And she often did as a public speaker and at medical meetings.

At one American Medical Association meeting she was asked to discuss a paper on Frigidity in Women. The meeting had been a particularly serious-minded one. The papers presented were all long and scholarly, documented by a great deal of data.

The various discussions were equally long and scholarly. Mother's contribution had been left to the very end, and she noticed that her audience was visibly fatigued by the intellectual exertions of the day. Not to put too fine a point on it, several people were sound asleep.

Mother woke them all up, by a very simple method. Her entire discussion of frigidity in women consisted of this masterly summing up of one school of thought on the matter.

"The reason so many American women are frigid," she said, "is because so many American men are *ausgespielt!*" And to a man, played out or not, the room, once it stopped laughing, gave her an ovation.

The Last Chapter—So Far

HERE SHE IS at the ripe old age of seventy-odd (and don't think my mother will admit either to the seventy or to the odd). When I first told her about the book, she had one comment to make: Just make it perfectly clear that I graduated from medical school at ten! At her recent fifty-fifth college reunion, she was adopted by the class of 1959, and came back from the reunion saying, "I don't understand why I'm the only one in *my* class who's only fifty!" But age cannot deter her nor custom stale her excitement at the possibilities of medicine or her determination to upset a *status quo* that she considers anti-feminine, unfair, or unjust.

In her seventies, she started a brand-new career. One of her patients came to her about two years ago in a state of great agitation. She was terribly concerned about her son who, she first explained to my mother, "had gotten into a bad crowd." For a while my mother soothed her with explanations about the generation gap, the new culture, and other clichés of the late sixties. Then it was borne in upon my mother that the "bad crowd" included a friendly neighborhood dope pusher and that her patient had very real troubles.

The boy was sixteen. He had developed a $75-a-day habit.

He was mainlining and he wanted out. He had tried various methods of kicking the habit by himself. But between his "friends," the dope pusher (who had a nasty habit of giving him "just one more before you kick it"), and the psychological hangups that had started him on dope to begin with, he wasn't having a great deal of success.

Through the intervention of counselors in his school, he was persuaded to turn himself in and go into the rehabilitation program at Lexington. My mother congratulated her patient, prescribed some tranquilizers for *her,* and even saw the boy herself during his waiting period. The waiting period for voluntary rehabilitation stretched on and on. The tranquilizers my mother prescribed became more and more potent. And one day the boy, tired of waiting in a world that seemed not to care, hanged himself.

My mother had a new crusade.

She started out treating people who were waiting for admission to Lexington. Then the word began getting around. Here was a doctor who was giving out prescriptions that would normally cost you lots of money. And all it cost was a few dollars a week. Slowly but surely her marriage-counseling patients were squeezed out by the crush of waiting dope addicts. Slowly but surely her gynecological patients got tired of having their pocketbooks stolen while they were waiting.

Meanwhile, Mother was experimenting. She evolved a system of treatment that—as she phrased it—leaves them no more hooked than the rest of America's take-a-pill society. It was something to put them to sleep at night. Something to wake them up in the morning, and something to take if they find they can't get through the day. It worked. Men who hadn't been able to do anything but steal enough to get from one shot to another suddenly began functioning in jobs, and —as they hadn't for years—in their homes as husbands and fathers. Mother was jubilant. Here was a wonderful new phase of medicine.

That was in the very beginning. Then things began to change.

First came the change in her patients. More and more of them seemed less and less interested in getting to Lexington. More and more began begging for a fix, offering her "big money."

After a little of this, she took one big step. She picked up her hat and her narcotics license, and went off to the local police station.

"Yes, lady," said the sergeant, "what can we do for you?" He clearly expected her to complain about a man under her bed or a snatched purse.

"I want to turn in my narcotics license. I'm Dr. Daniels."

The sergeant was totally nonplussed. "But what are we going to do with your license, Doctor?" he asked.

"I don't know. But I do know that if I can dispense narcotics, and a patient comes and begs long enough and plausibly enough, I'll give it to him. So I'm turning in my license."

"Well, you can't give it to me. Wait a minute."

And after repeating this interview with about five or six people, she finally left the license in charge of a very puzzled detective.

In two days she was back.

"Hi, Doctor," said the sergeant, "you've come back for your license?" He seemed relieved.

"No," said Mother, "I want to talk to someone about how you people treat narcotics addicts."

The sergeant knew a hot potato when he faced one. He got rid of her, fast.

The next person she talked to at the police station said: "What do you mean, 'how do we treat narcotics addicts?' We arrest them. How else can we treat them?"

"Well," said Mother, "that's exactly what I want to know. How else can you treat them? They are coming to me by the hundreds. They are begging for treatment. They can't get into the experimental projects that get all the publicity. Everyone treats them like criminals. What can I do for them?"

Obviously this was not a problem the local police station could solve. She went to the County Medical Society, which sent her to the special state and federal narcotics divisions, which sent her all over. None of them seemed to have any constructive suggestions, but they all agreed that the way she was treating addicts ("catering to them, making it easy") was all wrong.

She tried one or two of the therapeutic suggestions that had been made to her. She says: "What they're trying to do is poison these people. All those treatments do is make them even sicker than the drugs."

Determinedly she went back to her own course of treatment, which at least let her patients function. Then things began to happen with a vengeance.

Since her office was on a high floor of an apartment house, the tenants began protesting. With dope addicts in the elevators, they didn't feel safe going in and out. The first time my mother went to court was to answer a complaint from the tenants and the landlord trying to evict her.

That was thrown out of court.

Next she had a visit from two men claiming to be narcotics agents. She had her doubts. She had, after all, been receiving frequent visits from practically resident narcotics agents who kept saying to her in despair: "Why does a nice old lady like you want to have a practice like this? Go back to treating other ladies." The first one came in posing as a patient. The next came in posing as a police officer, and saying: "Give us some money and we won't have your license taken away. Otherwise we will."

"Well," said my mother, thinking they certainly weren't anything like *her* policemen and narcotics agents, "I can give you twenty dollars. That's all I have on me."

"You're kidding," said the supposed policeman, "I need at least three hundred."

"Well," said Mother, thinking fast, "I can give you a check or you can come back for the money this afternoon."

"I'll be back, and you'd better have it," said the supposed policeman, suddenly sounding very menacing.

The minute he walked out, my mother called her lawyer and the friendly desk sergeant. But, of course, the pseudopoliceman never did come back.

The next week one of her patients held her up at knife-point.

"Where's the stuff?" he asked, jabbing at her side.

"Don't you think I know you better than to keep anything here? I haven't got any narcotics; I can't prescribe any narcotics. I'm trying to help you. I won't keep you on that poison, you know that."

Since no amount of jabbing would change her story, she lost that particular patient without regret.

Gradually she noticed that all the bric-a-brac in her office was disappearing. Then the waiting-room rug (twenty-five feet by fifteen feet) vanished. The room began to have a very barren look.

She acquired a large police dog who slept behind her desk during office hours. But since she had no time to walk him, that chore was taken over by her patients. This rendered him something less than useful as a watchdog.

More and more objects evaporated from the office. She was held up again and again—at knifepoint and at gunpoint. Her answer to the outraged expostulations of our whole family were always the same. "It's not my *good* patients that are holding me up."

"So," we all said, "why not treat just the good ones?"

"You think I can tell from looking which are the good and which are the bad? And I never know when a bad will turn good. When they come to me, society has said they're all 'bad.'

They're outcasts. And look what I can do for them. Am I supposed to say to this one and that one—you and you, you're bad. I don't care that you're sick. I won't treat you. Can I do that? After all, am I a doctor or aren't I?"

"Mother," we said, "you're going to get killed. One of these days a gun will go off, and you'll get shot."

"What better way is there for an old lady to die than doing good for desperate people, and practicing medicine as it should be practiced, really healing the sick?" We knew there was no point in arguing any further. If she was willing to admit she was old, it was a cause she would never give up.

She was called before the County Medical Society, who, bedazzled by the two bows she wore in her hair, her hippy sandals, and the long time it took her lawyer to read her write-up in a medical who's who reserved judgment on her case. She returned home from the trial to find that one of her patients had managed to set fire to her apartment and all but burn her out.

And that's where it stands now. Although she has given up treating dope addicts, the Attorney General is still after her. Her ex-patients seem to have her pegged for a weekly holdup. And she stands gaily, behind boarded windows, triumphantly Hannah, Anna, Anna Kleegman Daniels—my mother, the doctor.

Glossary

ausgespielt—played out, tired out
beshert—fated
Borsha moya—my God
briss—ritual circumcision
gay avec—go away
gelt—money
goldene medina—literally, golden land; colloquially, the promised land
gonif—thief
goy—Christian (noun)
goyim—Christians
goyische—Christian (adjective)
hoopah—the ceremonial canopy held over a bride and groom
huzzadiche—literally, garbagey; colloquially, lousy
ich—I
ja—yes
kibitz—give unwanted advice
kind—child
kleine—small, little
koyech—strength, courage, will to survive
kunstwerk—masterpiece
kvass—a soft drink

Lachiam toiveem sholem—To life (a toast); to the good life and the life of peace

landtsman—townsman, countryman

lox—smoked salmon, usually eaten with bagels

maidele—young girl

mann—man

mazeltov—lucky day, congratulations

mein—my

meshugenahs—crazy people, nuts

mespucha—a family with all the relations included

mikveh—the ceremonial bath at which women are cleansed

na—no

nacht—night

oi—exclamation of despair or joy

oi, bist ir a gonif—oh, what a thief he is

oi guttenu—O my God

pais—the ritual curls, never cut, of an orthodox Jewish man

Pesach—Passover

Pesadiche—for Passover

pogrom—anti-Semitic riot

proshenya—proclamation

reb—rabbi, wise man (often as honorary title denoting learning)

schon—okay, also fine, handsome, a multipurpose word equivalent to a hippy "beautiful"

Seder—the Jewish spring feast to celebrate Passover. It falls around Easter

sha—be quiet

Shabbus—the Jewish sabbath, from sundown Friday to sundown Saturday

Shabbus by nacht—eve of the Sabbath

shagetz—a Christian man

shaine—beautiful, handsome

shaittel—the wig an orthodox Jewish woman wears after marriage

shiddach—a match made by a matchmaker, any engagement

sholem—peace, hello, good-bye. An all-purpose salutation
shul—a Jewish temple or synagogue
shunde—a scandal
stetl—a small Jewish town
tauchterle—little daughter, little child
trefe—unkosher, unclean
veiss—know
vierst—a Russian unit of distance equal to .6629 miles
vus veiss ich—what do I know?
wunder—wonder
yeshivabucher—a learned rabbinical student